THE VATICAN'S SNAKEHEAD AUDITORIUM

- IS THE BLACK RACE DESTINED TO RULE THE NEW AGE?

THE VATICAN'S SNAKEHEAD AUDITORIUM

- IS THE BLACK RACE DESTINED TO RULE THE NEW AGE?

TUNJI ADEEKO

The Author of

THEY LIED TO US

– *Unveiling How Christianity and Islam Religions Were Forged.*

Copyright @ 2020 Tunji Adeeko

ISBN:

978-978-979-205-4 (paperback)

978-978-979-206-1 (hardcover)

978-978-979-207-8 (e-book)

Published by: **ABOMA GLOBAL CONCEPT ENT.**
P. O. Box 2098, Ikeja General Post Office,
Lagos State, Nigeria
West Africa
mailto:abomagc@rocketmail.com

website: www.tunjiadeeko.com

DEDICATION

To all lovers of truth
and those who crack
secret codes.

ACKNOWLEDGEMENTS AND APPRECIATION

All praises to the Infinite Creator,
and the numerous helpers that
inspired and revealed all secrets.

Everything came to the light
because the right
time has come.

ABOUT THE AUTHOR

The world is filled with many religions and monotheism, that is, the faith in only one-God, claims roughly half of the world population. Monotheistic religions are Judaism, Christianity, Islam, and many other branches of the Abrahamic faith. These religions were created mainly in the Middle East and then spread across the Western World, Latin America, and Africa with little success in the Far East.

As a young African Prince, growing up in my town in South-West Nigeria, I would often wonder in my teen ages how I would rule over my people, if and when called upon to do so. My grave concern was not unconnected with the multiple religions in the land and its devastating effect on the Africans. The drive to find accurate answers to the origin of the belief that there is one God in heaven, yet so variously displayed by the three Abrahamic religions, and in others, is the impetus for my search.

I aim to uncover and share the truth about humankind's origin, the purpose of human existence, and the future of the world as much as I can. I hope this truth would raise human consciousness because a global revitalisation and transformation of human minds are speedily underway. The earth is in dire need of true human heroes and heroines to save her.

I have only written two books:

THEY LIED TO US – Unveiling How Christianity and Islam Religions Were Forged.

THE VATICAN'S SNAKEHEAD AUDITORIUM
– The Old Warlord Is Back To Power! (Free e-book Edition)

THE VATICAN'S SNAKEHEAD AUDITORIUM
– Is The Black Race Destined To Rule The New Age?

EDITORIAL COMMENT

ISBN 978-978-968-841-8
(e-book)

ISBN 978-978-968-840-1
(Paperback)

For details about the
book availability, visit

www.tunjiadeeko.com

Dear Tunji,

"Thank you for the opportunity to help you with your most interesting, enthralling, and informative manuscript. With such ardent, passionate, and tenacious zeal to uncover what is true and lay bare what is false, you have written a thoroughly researched and credible book that will, I think, open many peoples' eyes and minds, but is also likely to stir up much controversy, as you well know! I, for one, have certainly learnt so much of real value and have gained an expanded perspective and understanding of many things whilst working on it, even though I am very much in alignment and agreement with your beliefs."

— Franklin **Kartun**
Reach Publishers, South Africa

CONTENTS

PREFACE TO THE NEW EDITION

An African proverb says, "If lie travels for a thousand years, one day the truth would catch up with it." I started in February 2020 to use the content of my free e-book titled THE VATICAN'S SNAKEHEAD AUDITORIUM – *The Old Warlord Is Back To Power!* to announce the arrival of my long-awaited book, THEY LIED TO US.

No sooner had I start, the universe begins to inundate me with revelations. The secrets are so unique, and I had no choice but to embrace, appreciate, and share it. These revelations came in the form of connecting more dots than I had ever imagined or ever knew existed. Some of the information also came from unexpected sources. What I shared on Facebook was, in many ways, much more profound than what I put down in the free e-book. There and then, I knew that an enlarged edition was, in a matter of time, a necessity.

It would be inappropriate for anyone to imagine that the primary purpose of writing this book is to expose a group of people called the Freemasons or Illuminati. No, that's far beside the main issue. When the Vatican built a reptilian-looking Audience Hall in Italy in 1971, they inadvertently reveal a big secret, and they dare the world to reason it out and know the truth behind it. If the truth is now coming out via this book, I believe that the universe wishes it.

Tunji Adeeko
September 2020

PREFACE TO THE FREE E-BOOK

The Paul VI Audience Hall, also known as the Hall of the Pontifical Audiences, is situated partly in Vatican City and Rome, Italy. I became aware of the existence of this Hall two years after I had submitted the manuscript of my book, THEY LIED TO US, to a publisher. Upon sighting its pictures, I searched the internet profusely for any clue as to what meaning scholars or the public could have alluded to it. Many were baffled that the features are unmistakably reptilian. Some are quick to observe that whatever it is, it contradicts the Bible's teachings, which without ambiguity, called Satan or Lucifer a Serpent or Dragon. The closest explanation proffered is that the Vatican was long associated with the ancient secret society called the Brotherhood of the Snake. This group, over the years, has produced many occult-based organisations. According to a comment credited to Maggie Eriksson, Pastor, Bible Scholar-Teacher, Christian Counselor on Quora, she says that "the word "Vatican" literally means "Divining Serpent," and is derived from **Vatis** = Diviner and **Can** = Serpent." Others say the meaning has to do with "to prophesy" or "oracle." However, Merriam-Webster dictionary says the word was borrowed from Latin (mons) Vāticānus - a hill on the west bank of the Tiber. Another comment on Quora also concludes thus, "Common sense would suggest that they wanted to congregate at an altar dedicated to the snake." It is alleged, in some quarters, that the earth is under the control of a reptilian race and that the origin of the reptilian races is extraterrestrial.

In THEY LIED TO US, I followed the path laid out by the late Zechariah Sitchin and many great authors. I reviewed human history from the standpoint of alternative science advocators. They believe and explain that some astronauts called Anunnaki visited the earth about half a million years ago. (In some instances, the period when space rockets were visiting the earth planet has been proven to be more than one billion years. Therefore, before the Anunnaki, it is established that many other species of extraterrestrials (ETs) visited the earth.) As the story goes, the Anunnaki were more ambitious than the other ETs. They tampered with and crossbred their species with the hominids present on earth to produce the intelligent humans, Homo sapiens sapiens. They also became the prehistoric gods and goddesses of Sumer, Akkad, Egypt, India, the earliest ancestors that the Chinese worshipped, and so on.

If Zechariah Sitchin, in particular, was right, I wanted to take his work further and garnish the Anunnaki's story with the latest information I could get. There are apparent omens I expected Mr Sitchin to identify and mention, but he was utterly silent on them. For example, if 3,800 – 3,760 BCE were 40-years Nibiru Window as his writings imply, one would expect that 200 – 160 BCE should be another window since the Nibiru (the Anunnaki planet) orbit follows a 3,600-year elliptical path (trajectory) around our Sun. On this critical point where Sitchin was silent, I discovered that Josephus long spoke. By carefully studying the works of Flavius Josephus, thanks to Abelard Reuchlin, who linked Josephus and his family (nuclear and extended) to the authorship of the New Testament. I discovered that the supposed first-century Jewish historian indeed alluded a possible window at a date corresponding to 200 – 160 BCE. According to Sitchin, this window is when the larger council of the Anunnaki visits the earth to review human progress and the activities of the assigned Anunnaki team on Earth Mission.

I submitted in THEY LIED TO US that it was Enlil – the head of the Sumerian pantheon - and his family, in the sixth century BCE, which snatched the Jews from the

Babylonia Captivity. They fabricated a remarkable history for the Jewish nation. In that concocted story, Adam and Eve were falsely regarded as the first human couple, created circa 3,760 BCE according to the chronology established in the Jewish scripture. And the supposed sin of the first couple formed the bedrock upon which the Messiah story in the monotheistic religion (faith in one-God) became necessary. Enlil and his family did this to outwit his elder brother, Enki, and Marduk, alongside their lineage. Until the end of the Babylonia era, the Enki dynasty was headed by Enki's first son Marduk. He was ruling the world from Babylon alongside his son Nabu under a religious ideology that could best be described as henotheism - the worship of one god while acknowledging the existence of other gods. The larger members of the Enki's family, with their scribes and priests, were ruling Egypt and Africa at large. '

In Babylon, which used to be a top centre of activities for the Sumerian and Akkadian Empire, all the olden Anunnaki gods and goddesses were forbidden. They were restricted to remote shrines. Marduk, during that Age (of Aries), 2020 BCE – 140 CE, was recognised as the king and lord of the gods and goddesses. His name was substituted for Nibiru and Enlil as the slaughterer of a primaeval mythological dragon called Tiamat in an ancient document called Enûma eliš. The Bible also mentioned this dragon.[1]

The visiting Anunnaki council, during the last Nibiru Window of 200 – 160 BCE, judging by the events that followed that period, rejected the Enlilites' plan to use the Jews to rule the oncoming New Age (of Pisces). Instead, the Romans were taken. In place of Jerusalem, Rome was chosen. In Rome's efforts to implement the new directive or Order From Above, Rome changed the lunar calendar that was hitherto in use since the days of the ancient Greek and

---

[1] Psalms 89:10, Isaiah 51:9

earliest days of Rome, to the solar calendar. The solar cosmic timing was invented in Egypt, and further fine-tuned circa 4,236 BCE. Also, numerous obelisks were transferred from Egypt to Rome to decorate her new status as the new 'BABYLON THE GREAT.'[2] Several obelisks liter the earth today. They are the sign of allegiance to the reigning family, and in some cases, as a remnant of the old warlord's influence.

When I realised that a well-orchestrated game plan was well underway, I reviewed the general history. I identified that the Jewish Return from Babylonia Captivity was more of a political effort than a spiritual renewal of the Jewish nation - a wrong belief among the Bible readers. While the making of Christianity was underway, the Septuagint, the Greek version of the Hebrew Bible, was carefully adulterated. The contamination was introduced via the misconstruction of Hebrew words or phrases to accommodate a possible appearance in the 'first' century of a "Messiah the Prince" or an 'Angel Messiah' as Ernest de Bunsen put it. The closing of the New Testament was reportedly dragged into the second (and possibly fourth) century CE with many details added, deducted, and backdated as those in authority deemed fit. For this reason, the original New Testament manuscript dated to the first century may never be found.

I carefully used obscure Bible passages, extracts from Zechariah Sitchin's writings, and the Church history to uncover that the time allotted to Jesus Christ was never the beginning of an Age or a 'first' century as it is now popularly imagined. Instead, that period was the end of the Age of Aries, which expired circa 140 CE. The Bible writers knew this and cleverly manipulated facts and history. The removal of the Jews from Palestine in 132 – 136 CE following a revolt led by Bar Kokhbar was a political

---

[2] Revelation 17:5, 18:2

struggle initiated to exterminate the Jews from Palestine. This became necessary to clear the way, not for Christianity or Jesus Christ but the Romans. The Romans, after they had successfully invented Christianity, effectively began to rule the Age of Pisces from 140 CE without any threat from Judaism. Unknown to many Bible readers, it was never the individuals whose name appears on the cover of the books of the New Testament or the imaginary disciples who wrote the Messiah's story but the Roman aristocrats. The authors of the New Testament were smart enough to put their signature across the Bible verses and chapters in the form of numerical symbols. All these revelations are for the pleasure of the reader of my book - THEY LIED TO US.

I also discovered that four different years allude to the birth of Jesus Christ. The authors of three dates are Daniel (3BCE), Matthew (6BCE), and Luke (AD 7). For the Church to establish Jesus' birth, ministry, and time as an event that took place in the "first" century, the monk who worked at a complex that was later named the Vatican, in the 6th century, used the different dates mentioned in Matthew and Luke to invent the *Anno Domini* calendar. This act led to the creation of Jesus Christ's fourth birth date, AD 1. The simple tact adopted by the monk was to pick the middle point of the 13 years difference between the year of birth mentioned by 'Matthew' and 'Luke.' The general Bible believers, the sheep, who are led by the numerous shepherds, are unaware of the behind-the-scenes manipulations that went into the making of the book they accepted by 'faith' as a holy book. Those who knew kept mute, rode on a "Greek gift" and enjoyed the booty 'sacrifices' offered by the laymen and religious followers to enrich self and "ministry" while waiting for a Jesus Christ who would return in the year *infinity.*

The fallouts from these discoveries are that: the 'prophecy' concerning the virgin birth of a Messiah in the 'first' century (Virgo was derived from astronomy), Jesus' four birth dates, Jesus' ministry alongside 12 disciples (representing Jesus as the Sun, surrounded by the 12 zodiac signs to make the 13-member principal team), Jesus' death on Nisan 13th (recorded by John) and 14th (recorded by Synoptic Gospels), and the resurrection details which do not fit into Good Friday and Easter Sunday festivals that the world observes till date – all these forced a sincere seeker in me to come to a profound conclusion. That conclusion is simply this: The story of Jesus Christ was never factual; it was fabricated. There is no legacy of Jesus Christ in human history to date other than things attributed to him, which, when carefully scrutinized, never originate from him either in words or practice but stolen for him from ancient history and religious traditions.

In THEY LIED TO US, I utilised the revelations found in the ancient Sumerian texts, Astronomy (and Astrological Age), Bible, and Maya Long Count calendar to retell the human history, collaboratively and to conclude that a historical Jesus never existed. If I ever had any reservation(s) in my submission, I found a melting point in the reptilian edifice at the Vatican. This highly compelling structure fits as a natural capstone on my (then) unpublished work showcasing the height and completion of all ancient mysteries. In this magnificent but highly symbolic building is the answer that human beings are not in control of the earth. Human destiny is under a remote control system since time immemorial, with the real players hidden away from the masses.

It also brings to the fore the arguments that religions were invented by the Anunnaki to create a false concept, false hope, and enslave humankind in a colony called earth. For those who are well-read on this subject matter, most of the things I brought out are not new in its entirety. I might have only reshuffled and rearranged the puzzles to tell the old story in a new light. Therefore, for those who are reading these things for the first time, my two books would provide an overwhelming opportunity to know the hidden-truth of how and why they fabricated monotheistic religions about 2,500 years ago. Also, updates on the Anunnaki's change in leadership in the 14th century and its effect on the fate of humankind the reader would find very compelling. In the Vatican Snakehead symbols and the correct interpretations, the age-long truth (the real ancient human history) hitherto misrepresented as ancient myths are now revealed. In contrast, the popular myth, up till now presented as Gospel truth, is now exposed as "a pious fraud."

On Facebook, I posted a rhetorical question while the Vatican's snakehead auditorium pictures were on display, saying – If the serpent represents Satan according to the Bible, what moral does the Mother Church at the Vatican have in building a magnificent monument in its honour? It is either that the Vatican is worshipping Satan or Lucifer, as some concerned groups of people have alleged, or that the serpent story in the Bible was never literal but an allegory. This book is set to proffer an answer to the riddle.

It is essential to state that I focus on using the Bible to drive my points on the global monotheistic religions because I understood the three religions of Judaism, Christianity, and Islam, as the offshoot of astronomy. Christianity represents the Sun - she uses a solar calendar and carries her flock to worship on a Sun-day. On the other hand, Judaism represents the moon with the star of David. This ideology was later transferred to Islam since the Jewish nation no longer existed in Palestine in the 7th century. Islam continued with using a lunar calendar and displayed the moon crest with a star (the symbol of Nibiru) to the world to see. The moon has no light by itself except that which the Sun casts on it.

The main contents of the Qur'an, therefore, are revised biblical stories and experiences carefully domiciled in Jewish sister language and culture, the Arabic. Hence, the Anunnaki, ruling from the Vatican, intricately derived Qur'an from the fabric of Judaism and Christianity. The two religions of Christianity and Islam, without any doubt, are two sides of a coin. And this coin was minted by the old Sumerian/Egyptian/Babylonian gods and goddesses, which metamorphosed into the assumed ONE GOD of today. They fabricated the original Jesus story and replicated the information in the hand of the prophet from Arabia to produce the Qur'an.

Tunji Adeeko
September 2019

Introduction

THE ELITES AND THE MASSES

*"YOU are a migratory soul, inhabiting a
physical body to share in the earth's great
experience – a path you knew about before
you were born, yet, you chose to forget so that
you could rediscover your true self. Each
soul's power grows with what it discovers."*

The soul of human beings has a designated path, and this path or destiny, as it is often called, may be found and satisfied, or a misstep might cause a derailment. When destiny is derailed, the journey to earth becomes compromised, giving rise to a failed mission. In my book, THEY LIED TO US, I explained that the chief causes of the soul's failure are predominantly 'ignorance' and 'distractions.'

Ignorance is the inability of an individual to come to terms that the greatest treasure and guide in the soul's earth's mission is the natural "compass" deposited in everyone. This compass exhibits itself through the mechanism called MIND. It utilises personal 'gifts' such as instincts, inner voice, dreams, discernment, trance-like experiences, visions, prophecy, and the Free Will to navigate the maze of life. All these are natural abilities though some are classified as extrasensory experiences. These natural gifts are deposited differently in individuals based on capability and tasks to accomplish in life. The mind, therefore, serves as the engine room where thoughts and information are processed. It also links the physical body to the larger world called the universe. When the mind is healthy, the spirit is healthy, and then the physical body is expected to be healthy.

Secondly, through the mind, knowledge is acquired. In every human being across the world, different gifts are deposited. Therefore, the primary task of the human race is to collate various experiences and form synergy by tapping from the best brains available to solve practical problems. However, when individuals or a society played down on diversity of gifts and refused to cross-fertilise their minds with the new and ever-renewed minds across the globe, they become disfranchised, redundant, and non-progressive. In the absence of sharp and progressive minds, fear and superstitions set in.

Distractions, on the other hand, are the obstacles, either natural or created, false ideologies generated by the global elites, and planned to impede the path of every earth sojourner. Sources of distractions include religion, education/training, ethnic/tribal beliefs, philosophies, entertainments, reprobate practises, etc. As soon as an individual dwells in ignorance, a distracted and crooked pathway becomes a natural abode, limiting a person's potentials. Ignorance and distractions are used by the regional or global elites to keep human souls from growing unto a higher plane. Souls are, therefore, grounded to earth or earth-like realms, where they serve the masters of the 'evil' world.

Man is not alone in the universe. Other beings exist and operate in their worlds at various realms and levels of the evolution ladder or state of consciousness. They are found in and around the earth, on different planets within the Milky Way, and in other galaxies. Some of these worlds run simultaneously with and within human space. This is made possible because we all operate at different frequencies. Over the years in human history, there is copious evidence of meddling between humans and these "foreigners" who are earth visitors and intruders or the

Unidentified Living Neighbours.[3] The relationships between humans and these beings could be beneficial or parasitic, depending on whether the parties involved are benevolent or malevolent. Also, it depends on which side of the divide an individual aligns - good or evil. The activities of the myriads of visible or extrasensory-only-perceived-neighbors sometimes account for the work of geniuses, business and technology transfers, religious miracles, and evil in human society.

In some cases, however, the relationship might be neutral where one's party's needs and supplies do not interfere with that of the other parties. Everyone merely coexists in their respective realms or abode. Humankind ignorantly refers to encounters with these beings as intercourse with God, Satan, angels, demons, ancestral spirits, and 'spirits' under various terms. These spirit beings are considered as constituting "principalities and powers in high places." The misconception and wrong categorization sometimes arise due to misinform-mation borne out of ignorance or careful programming of the humans' minds.

Some humans are naturally gifted or could be trained to interact with these beings. Parapsychology is the study of supposed mental phenomena that cannot be explained by known psychological or scientific principles. The field study refers to individuals who specialise in the display of extrasensory perception or telepathy communications or any other forms of clairvoyance as 'channelers.' In spiritualism, they act as medium receiving messages from the "spirit beings of the universe." Some individuals are also natural channelers, which could be mistaken for brilliancy or high intelligence. High instabilities are upon

---

[3] 'Unidentified Living Neighbour' in the sense that the names, true nature and characters of the spiritual entities are never properly identified and documented.

the earth following the misinterpretation and abuse of this relationship and skills.

Humankind sometimes enters into multiple alliances with various beings, either as individuals or in groups – a family, village, or town, intentionally or ignorantly. This includes world leaders in multiple fields. Such unions negotiate for information, technology, riches, and power (be it political, demonic, or miraculous healings). The powers derived are, most of the time, used to oppress, manipulate, and subvert people's free will for personal aggrandisement. Only on a few occasions are the secret knowledge and power obtained from the many pacts with supernatural beings used to benefit humanity without an additional burden such as mental or religious slavery. In the search for affluence, influence, and power, many individuals, great and small, are reported to have sold their souls.

Some elites are hybrids of some extraterrestrial [ET] beings or humans recruited by the ETs. The elites knew that it would be tough to control the fast-growing masses without a careful plan. They are reputed as Master Planners or the Great Architect of the world. They probed and discovered that the human soul (spirit and mind) could be tamed and subjugated to a state of perpetual fear, guilt, and total dependency. This could be achieved via outright hypnotism or persistence and continuous thought suggestions through controlled education that supports memorisation instead of critical thinking, religious programming, etc.. The masses are, therefore, made to believe that they are educated and possess free will to make choices. In contrast, the observed reality has been twisted and highly influenced. Almost every field of human endeavours, such as religions, education, philosophy, and entertainment, is, therefore, controlled and monitored.

Next, they identified that to suppress local ideas, they needed to provide a foreign and attractive global view that the masses would never resist. In the alternative proposed and taught, humans would be made unaware of who they are or the true meaning of their origin and purpose. Therefore, the masses will accept whatever nomenclatures they are called and imbibe no personal ambition higher than what the elite groups have sanctioned and made possible. The masses would voluntarily relinquish all their powers to the Master Planners of the new idea and the foreign institutions that founded them. Hence, politics, religion, and government are established just as the elites wanted them to be. Unknown to the regional leaders, the global network is pyramidal, which channel all resources back to the foreign and unified elite masters at the top. Below them are small fraternities for religions, nations, tribes, businesses, games and leisure, entertainment, clubs, etc..

Typically, for any soul to be deemed successful on earth's mission, it must attain a zenith called enlightenment, or else the person repeats the unaccomplished task. The repeat journey may be on earth or other habitable planetary locations in the universe until the right lesson is learnt. Enlightenment could be self-taught or self-driven or nurtured by specially prepared mentors, formally or informally. The maxim is that when the student is ready, the universe will cause the teacher to appear. The 'teacher' may not necessarily have to be human beings; information could be exchanged via daytime or nighttime dreams, curious minds, memory flashes, red flags in the forms of audible voice or sounds, or seemly familiar faces or places, etc. People naturally become awake or self-conscious at different stages of life. The organised religions and specialized school of mysticism had usurped this natural rebirth process, substituting the elite's conscious-ness for universal consciousness to slow down the pace of human growth.

The enlightened souls are those who are firmly at alert and follow their instincts to gain understanding into the available pathways in the universe. Also, they use their sharp mind to attract knowledge to know what is right and proper, separated from various falsehoods. They are never afraid to ask questions to gain insight into the complex human nature void of earthly politics. They might first understand that there is more to life than what is available in the public domains. Sometimes, they readily agree that there are Hidden Hands that are controlling human destiny. Their awareness sometimes transcends physical life experiences into understanding spiritual or metaphysical mysteries. Most of the time, they make conscious efforts to pull out of the crowd and learn and know certain secrets with total clarity. They seek to know 'what is working' instead of following the masses to believe that 'God' or 'Government' or 'The Power That Be' holds exclusive powers in determining what would work and what would not work.

The path taken to achieve enlightenment differs from one individual to another. The state of awareness and the subsequent growth may be fast, reasonable, retarded, or zero, depending on an individual's readiness and time of awakening. Zero response should not be misconstrued that a particular human being does not have a soul. Though, this could be the case for genetically manipulated half-robotic half-human or artificial intelligence beings. Instead, it means that the individual concerned, for whatever reason, never grew or refused to grow. The 'seed of life' was never provided with the good ingredients (the right information and mental alertness) required to wake it up from dormancy (the state of forgetfulness) to express its unique traits and beauty. It is like a butterfly egg that would not grow to become a larva; hence, it could not become an adult to spread its beautiful wings and display the magnificence beauty. Many are chameleon-like; they live and adapt to whatever they see, hear, and feel to please others. They become everything other than their true self, and sometimes, they forgot what their true self could have ever been.

The path to enlightenment often starts with these words – WHO AM I? WHY AM I HERE? Only those who came up with the right answers become awakened and subsequently enlightened. For an individual to come to maturity requires tenacity and hard work built layers upon layers after seeking and knowing aright. Many hold unto answers provided for them and not the one that comes from deep within if they had been sincere in their search. Self-discovery is not a one day or one-off scenario; it is a lifetime pursuit. The journey may not be rosy all the time, but the wisdom acquired is sufficient to satisfy a searching soul.

The non-awakened and unenlightened people are those who put in their best to comply with the falsified earth system. They assume that the world exists at its best; hence, there is no need to change or challenge anything. They belong to one of the groups of the six blind men who visited and touched an elephant, they described the elephant in different ways, and each went about believing that whatever perception or reality they created about the elephant, so and true it is. Although all their views are at a significant disparity from one to another, and what the elephant is, none is willing to admit that they could be wrong. In THEY LIED TO US, I identified the six groups of blind men who have now built mammoth followership that constitute the human population as **Hinduism, Buddhism, Christianity, Islam** (cum Judaism), **Traditional beliefs,** and **Atheism** (cum Agnosticism).

The unenlightened souls are highly instrumental in promoting the fabricated lies of the hidden masters, with enormous funding and personal sacrifices, consciously or unconsciously. They, on the one hand, are prone to being myopic, radicals, activists, ethnically biased, violent, and wicked. On the other hand, some are shallow, mentally lazy, complacent, government apologetics, and fearful, never ready to rock any boat. Hence, they are easy tools for easy brainwash. They are frequently used to keep humanity perpetually disorganised and enchained.

In the classical work of Plato's allegory of the cave, he rightly explained how ideas and practices that the masses are holding on to are often a shadow of the truth. Over the ages, the elites have perfected the act of mass human mind control. According to Plato, the earth is like a cave (a colony), where controlled ideologies are churned out as believable facts within the formal or informal education systems. To become wise, everybody must philosophise, and to philosophise is to query *everything*. The elites envisaged all these, and they reasoned that when people are at peace and well-fed, they would, in many cases, begin to ask questions and query the constituted authorities and become conscious of the true nature of the Hidden Hand. To discourage such a gesture, it was necessary to create a perpetual state of tumult and lack. These have been achieved by intermittently crippling governments across many nations via ill-advised economic policies and debt burden, sponsored terrorism, inter and intra-tribal wrangling. Others include the breeding of corrupt leaders cum politicians. They manufacture diseases to induce epidemic or pandemic and then build a pharmaceutical industry and produce drugs and vaccines to manage the problems.

When a handful of people do eventually ask questions, what shall they be told and taught? When humans crave wants, who shall provide it? The elites, starting from the rear, positioned themselves primarily as the leading provider/supplier of vital human needs across different categories. They envisaged and planted themselves for an oligopolistic (global) economy driven by conglomerates. They developed processes whereby social demands are stimulated, and craving becomes essential, then fashion, and later addiction. This practice was necessary to guarantee continual business patronage and enormous profit. Here, the role of celebrities becomes very handy.

Humans are then made to believe that these actions define social status innately designed by fate and destiny to experience a particular lifestyle, even when it is dangerous and harmful to their health. Free will is sometimes grossly abused. They are made accustomed to the idea that GOD somewhat made them the way they are; hence, there was no need to change anything. In some cases, individuals manipulate their natural configurations, physical and physiological wellbeing. Such as in the cases of transgender or bizarre body modifications.

The Elite dread competition. Whenever anyone outside the approved group successfully reasons out big innovative ideas that may threaten their dominance, the elites will step in and buy it off at an attractive price. They sometimes carefully eliminate stubborn but bright inventors who would not sell. Or they make his work pale into insignificance by barring it from exposure via the controlled social network and available distribution platforms. Sometimes the inventor is frustrated and becomes a miserable person because the invention is never patented. The individual is deprived of funds required to develop the product or idea into any meaningful state. In some extreme cases, the elite fabricates a false accusation against the individual resulting in a legal matter and false convict; thus, he ends up in jail. The brightest of the masses are allowed to hold a franchise or become a vendor to the elites. At the zenith of every field of human life are seated the elite comfortably, checking on everyone for whosoever would dare to cross the lines. They are the KEEPPer of Secrets and the true shepherds of the masses.

Uncontrolled childbirth is a direct consequence of unchecked libido. This is further enhanced due to ignorance, illiteracy, poverty, and the biological expansion of religions. The ensued huge population put tremendous pressure on available resources. Couple with human gluttony tendencies, greed, and materialism, the state of imbalance and scarcity is heightened, which sometimes requires special pricing to widen the gap from the haves and have not's. These gestures result in inflation, and if not curtailed, hyperinflations. With time, the human becomes selfish and lack empathy. They develop hatred, strife, violence, crimes, and killings. Amid the chaotic situations, man is directed to cry unto the government or God. When a man runs to the secret societies or religious houses to connect with God, he meets the priests. These are the offspring of the original priests created by the elite. Unknown to many, it was the elite that created the "holy books" for religious purposes and cleverly manipulated the information about its origin to conceal their identity.

The religious books are manuals to control believers to reason in a certain way. The masses are repeatedly told that the books were written or inspired by GOD, and they should defend it, if possible, with their life. The believers are taught to pump life's earnings and savings to propagate religious beliefs as 'the work of God' for a fantastic reward after death. Unknown to the multitude is the fact that *GOD never wrote a book or inspired any*. The so-called holy books were written by the world's most celebrated and biggest con men whose interest was to restrain and control what they term as the human race's excesses. As said earlier, the elites are generous to pen down their signatures across the pages of the scriptures. Only the wise readers would learn to identify such autographs and decode it.

Chapter One

THE MASONIC SIGNATURE IN THE BIBLE

When we look back in human history, religions have carefully been positioned to play significant roles. The reason for this is straightforward: when you control a person's religion, you contain their minds and entire life. It is for this reason that "shepherds" are appointed to keep the "sheep" within the fold lest they go astray to where they may become awakened and then abandon the fold. With the approved "holy books," the shepherds and the sheep are kept in check. Every soul lost, either to awakenings or radicalism, translates into a loss of revenue for the organised religions, loss of control, the fear of further negative influence, and possibly, terrorism.

Since this book is about finding a plausible meaning to the reptilian building at the Vatican, the headquarters of the Mother Church, and the seat of the Pope, my first point of call is to use the Bible to search out why the reinforced edifice was built in 1971 after the foundation was laid in 1963 in Rome. To keep a record with the year when the foundation was set, it is a 6300 capacity building. When I searched for the word "SERPENT" using the electronic Bible, this is what I got:

1. After the poetic narration of the Elohist creation story in the book of Genesis chapter one, and the dramatic recount of the Jehovist creation version in Genesis, chapter two, the word 'Serpent' appears as the 3rd word in the 3rd chapter of the Bible. This finding exhibit the numerical character of '33.'

"Now the serpent..."[4]

There may or may not be anything unusual attached to this unique placement, but whenever the number "33" pops up, it is necessary to investigate it with utmost interest. Why? This number was long associated with secret societies such as the Freemason and Illuminati.

2. Another way the word "serpent" could be tagged in the Bible is "GEN 3:1" or just "31." A careful look at this number shows that a reverse order will become "13." Figure 13 is another number well associated with the same body mentioned in (1) above.

3. The phrase "Now the serpent" is made of **13 letters!**

From the above, the **first reference** to the word 'serpent' in the Bible threw up two specific numbers: 13 & 33. Let us keep this report in mind as I now make a parallel study into a major storyline in the New Testament:

4. Jesus Christ's ministry was primarily accomplished by his person alongside 12 disciples (1 + 12 = 13).

5. According to Matthew, Jesus was born two years before King Herod died in March, 4 BCE, that is, 6 BCE.

> *"Then Herod, when he saw that he was mocked of the wise men, was exceeding wroth, and sent forth, and slew all the children that were in Bethlehem, and in all the coasts thereof, from two years old and*

---

[4] Genesis 3:1

> *under, according to the time which he had*
> *diligently enquired of the wise men.*"[5]

However, Luke put the birth of the same Jesus in the days of Cyrenius as the governor of the province of Syria.

> *"And it came to pass in those days, that there*
> *went out a decree from Caesar Augustus,*
> *that all the world should be taxed. (And this*
> *taxing was first made when Cyrenius was*
> *governor of Syria.)* "[6]

With the help of Flavius Josephus, the supposed first-century Jewish historian, Emperor Augustus census that could have captured the Jews took place in the second year of Cyrenius' reign as the governor of the province of Syria, 7 CE. [Some authorities claimed that the taxation was carried out when Cyrenius was governor of Syria *the first time*. This explanation was provided to water down what appeared to be an apparent contradictory report between Mathew and Luke. However, it has long been proven that Cyrenius was never the governor of Syria when Herod was the king.]

From the above, therefore, there are **13 mysterious years** between the dates set down in Matthew and Luke. (In THEY LIED TO US, I have proven that this was never an error but a **13-year code** set for use by a future reviewer of the calendar. And that this information became handy when the *Anno Domini* calendar was invented in the 6th century.)

---

[5] Matthew 2:16
[6] Luke 2:1, 2

6. The date when Jesus was killed was put at Nisan 14 by the Synoptic Gospels, that is, the date when the Passover is traditionally eaten.[7] Jesus ate the Passover with his disciples in the evening of Nisan 14 and was killed during the daytime. The Jewish day is counted from sunset to sunset. However, the book of John contradicted the others and put the date of death at a day earlier - when the Passover was not yet eaten, the preparation of the Passover.[8] That is **Nisan 13.** This seemly contradiction was never an error; the purpose is to feature the number "13," the Masonic signature in the storyline.

7. Jesus Christ, according to Luke, commenced his ministry at about the age of thirty[9] and was killed in the "middle of a week" or the middle of seven years of prophecy, according to Daniel.

> *"And after threescore and two weeks shall Messiah be cut off, but not for himself:……*
> *And he shall confirm the covenant with many for one week: and in the midst of the week he shall cause the sacrifice and the oblation to cease,"* [10]

Therefore, Jesus supposedly caused "the sacrifice and the oblation to cease." His death was regarded to have put an end to the priestly sacrifices at the temple. He died according to prophecy "in the midst of the week" at 33 years old.

From the above, the birth, the ministry, and the death of Jesus Christ were carefully wrapped around the mysterious numbers, 13 & 33.

---

[7] Matthew 26:18, Mark 14:16, Luke 22:13
[8] John 18:28, 19:14
[9] Luke 3:23
[10] Daniel 9:26, 27

To crown it up, let us take a look at the American Great Seal and its unique features:

- 13 stars above the Eagle
- 13 steps on the Pyramid
- 13 letters in ANNUIT COEPTIS
- 13 letters in E PLURIBUS UNUM
- 13 vertical bars on the shield
- 13 horizontal stripes at the top of the shield
- 13 leaves on the olive branch
- 13 berries on the olive branch
- 13 arrows
- 33 feathers on the Eagle's right wing
- 33 feathers on the Eagle's left wing

Many were deceived that the grouping of the above-listed items in the 13s came about because the original American settlement had 13 colonies as at independence. This may be true, but was the 13 colonies by chance or intentional. Let us bear in mind that the Babylonians recognised only 12 constellations of stars when evidence abounds that there are more than that in the sky? They did this because number 6 was their basic unit of measurement. If the 13 had resulted from the number of the original colonies, what about the 33 feathers? Let us bear in mind that 33° Mason (Freemason) signifies a zenith in that organisation. Could that have been a coincidence too? Number 13 & 33, therefore, is Masonic signature in the Bible as found in the Old Testament, the New Testament, and in the symbol of a modern nation that protects that religion, the United States of America.

Further down in the creation story, the serpent, as one of the 'beasts of the field'[11] created by LORD God (Yahweh Elohim), paid an unscheduled visit to the first couple and caused endless ripples. In Genesis, the serpent was introduced as a very subtle creature, possessing unique

---

[11] Genesis 3:1

wisdom.[12] Hence, the serpent opened up the first woman for dialogue and cleverly led her to identify the only "thou shall not" instruction in the beautiful Pleasure Park called the Garden of Eden.[13] In the unguarded discussions that followed, the serpent inflated the ego in Mother Eve and made her see why it is a great idea to be as wise as the 'gods, knowing good and evil.'[14] The rest, as they say, is now history. Eve and then Adam ate from the tree, and the two were driven out of the Garden for disobedience. And, the serpent became accursed. According to the Bible, this was how evil and suffering were introduced into the world.

There is something very puzzling about Genesis 3:5 in the King James Version.

> *For God doth know that in the day ye eat thereof, then your eyes shall be opened, and ye shall be as **gods**, knowing good and evil.*

Why would the word **el-o-heem'** appear twice in a statement, and different translators would accord it different meanings? In the original Hebrew text, the statement appears as follows:

> *For **el-o-heem'** doth know that in the day ye eat thereof, then your eyes shall be opened, and ye shall be as **el-o-heem'**, knowing good and evil.*

According to Strong's Hebrew (430), the word 'elohîym (el-o-heem') is in plural and it could mean:

1) [**plural**]
    1a) rulers, judges
    1b) divine ones
    1c) angels

---

[12] Genesis 3:4,5
[13] Genesis 2:8,10, 15
[14] Genesis 3:5 (King James Version)

       1d) gods

2) **[plural intensive-singular meaning]**
    2a) god, goddess
    2b) godlike one
    2c) works or special possessions of God
    2d) the (true) God
    2e) God

Therefore, various Bible translators used different English words or phrases in the place of the second el-o-heem' in Genesis 3:5. These are:

    A. God[15]
    B. Gods[16]
    C. divine beings[17]
    D. gods[18]

The biggest challenge facing the Bible translators and the non-Hebrew reader is that how can one ascertain that an accurate translation has been done? While the enthusiastic Christian, of which I was once, would naturally assume that the plural nature el-o-heem' (translated as God) is a pointer to the presence of the Trinity at creation, it is doubtful if any Jew shared such enthusiasm.

As things are, and going by Strong's Hebrew, Genesis 1:1 could as well be translated as follows:

---

[15] New International Version (NIV), English Standard Version (ESV), New American Standard Bible (NASB), New Living Translation (NLT), American Standard Version (ASV), Darby Bible Translation (DBT), Christian Standard Bible (CSB), New King James Version (NKJV), etc.

[16] Douay-Rheims Bible

[17] NET BIBLE

[18] American King James Version (AKJV), Brenton Septuagint Translation (BST), Webster's Bible Translation (WBT), King James Version (KJV).

A. In the beginning God created the heaven and the earth.
B. In the beginning Gods created the heaven and the earth.
C. In the beginning, gods (and goddesses) created the heaven and the earth.
D. In the beginning,' divine beings' created the heaven and the earth.

Since we already detected the Masonic signature in the Genesis 3:1, could the phrase "…..and ye shall be as gods" as used by KJV and others be identified as an anachronism or a pointer to something much deeper? What could this more profound understanding of the Hebrew scripture be? Could it be that the writers of the Jewish scripture were aware of the polytheism that existed in the ancient world? In that case, it would be very rational to submit that *ab initio* there were many gods among the Sumerians, Egyptians, Indians, Babylonians, Assyrians, etc. and the Jews were not left out. However, Yahweh Elohim (LORD God) was considered the supreme among the pantheons, the king of the gods?

With the hindsight that the Babylonian chief god, Marduk, in the Age of Aries (2020 BCE – 140 CE), was given the same title of "the king of the gods." The Jews were a product of the Babylonian captivity and could have been fed with this notion. Hence, El of the Canaanites was most probably derived from the name of the Sumerian chief god, Enlil, who became the el-o-heem' of the Jews. Or, as argued from some quarters, Nanna, the son of Enlil, was the moon-god of the Canaanites, the Jews, and the Arab world. From Babylon Captivity, the pluralism of persons in the pantheon headed by Enlil metamorphosed into becoming the one God promoted in the succeeding Age of Pisces. The extended family of the gods and goddesses became the chief triad deities and the numerous "Saints" in the Catholic Church. For the same reason, in Islam, the pronoun for God or Allah could only be 'WE.'

Alternatively, if the statement is an anachronism, it signifies that when the 'serpent' spoke with Eve, she was an innocent creature of God and should never have known or conscious of the existence of multiple gods the serpent suggested. Or else, that the story as written in the Bible was written or compiled when the tales of the gods and goddesses of old were popular among humanity. This would indicate that the story was written during the Babylonia Captivity in the 6th-century BCE!

Whichever way we look at it, a careful searcher cannot but query if the story of Adam and Eve as the first human couple and the talking serpent in the Garden of Eden is a true story or an allegory, carefully penned and signed by the Masonic society?

Chapter Two

THE SERPENT IN JACOB'S PRAYER

The next place where the word "serpent" was used in the Bible is Genesis 49. The reader may wish to read the entire chapter. However, when the passage is viewed with a keen eye of a curious searcher, the following features are the underlining characters (KJV):

Reuben, unstable as water (vss. 3, 4) - **Aquarius,**

Simeon and Levi are brethren (vs. 5) – **Gemini,**

Judah is a lion's whelp (vs. 9) – **Leo,**

Zebulun shall dwell at the haven of the sea (vs. 13) – **Pisces,**

Issachar is a strong ass (vs. 14) – **Taurus,**

Dan shall be a *serpent*, an adder in the path (vs. 17) – **Scorpio,**

Gad, strong as ram (vs. 19) – **Aries,**

Asher his bread shall be fat, and he shall yield royal dainties [season of harvest] (vs. 20) – **Libra,**

Naphtali is a hind [female deer] (vs. 21) [associated with Christmas in December] – **Capricorn,**

Joseph is a bow, abode in strength (vss. 22 – 24) – **Sagittarius,**

Benjamin shall ravin as a wolf (vs. 27) – **Cancer,** and

The unnamed female, Dinah,[19] stands for a virgin, **Virgo,** that was defiled.

---

[19] Genesis 46:15

Without any doubt, astrology, as derived from the star constellations, was carefully preserved in the Bible. However, the Bible reader is told never to indulge in this practice[20] lest people turn around and worship the moon and the stars. Another question that comes to mind it this, now that we have dissected this passage and uncover the astronomical undertone, can we honestly believe that Jacob had twelve sons and a daughter totaling **13**-member offspring? Are Jacob characters and all written about him in the Bible a product of factual historical references or a legendary figure? The reader should note that the two verses where "Dan" was blessed and described as serpent and scorpion are 16 & 17. (16 + 17 = **33**.) The entire chapter in question has "**33**" verses.

In an argument put up after extensive research into the making of Christianity, Abelard Reuchlin[21] revealed that the original Bible text was written with verses. However, the verses were removed from the copies circulated among the masses. This was a careful way to delude the mind of the people so that the smart ones among them would not pick out the visible numerical signatures. However, when the time was ripe, just like in the *Anno Domini* calendar that put Jesus era in the "first" century, the complete work was released with verses and presented as if the verses were newly created.

---

[20] Deut. 4:19, 17:3; 2 King 23:5; Job 31:26, 27; Jer. 8:2; Ezek. 8:16; Amos 5:25-26
[21] Abelard Ruechlin: The True Authorship of The New Testament

Permit me to take an excerpt from my book THEY LIED TO US:

"Careful searchers have observed that while the Bible disclaims astrology, some events in the holy book are reflecting such topics.

The idolatrous reminiscence of the Israelites' life in Egypt was revisited in the (supposed) wilderness (experience) at the foot of Mount Sinai in the event of the molten golden calf, which depicts the Age of Taurus [the Bull] [4185 – 2025 BCE].

The Jewish book of Leviticus is chiefly about priestly traditions of the Levites and sacrificial rams, which depicts the Age of Aries [the Ram] [2024 BCE – 138/139 CE].

The Jews still celebrate an amazing Shofar Ram's Horn service to date.

The story of Jesus was filled with events and sayings about fishes and fishers, thus depicting the Age of Pisces [the Fishes] [140 – 2300 CE].

In the tail end of his ministry, Jesus was made to refer to a pitcher in Luke 22:10, thereby alluding to the next Age of Aquarius [the Water-bearer] [2300 – 4460 CE]."[22]

---

[22] Tunji Adeeko: THEY LIED TO US – Unveiling How Christianity and Islam Religions Were Forged, pg. 349

It is a fact that astronomy/astrology was not spared in the New Testament. As the Sun is surrounded by the twelve zodiac signs in our solar system, so was Jesus' ministry supposedly supported by twelve disciples. A smart reader would pick a fault in the above-stated statement because while the zodiac signs are twelve, there are thirteen characters. After all, the Gemini sign depicts the twins. This is true, and for this reason, the writer of the story gave "Jesus Christ" twelve male disciples and the immaculate virgin mother, the Virgo. In the zodiac, and particularly Gemini, the twins depict two different persons irrespective of sexes. Still, the two fishes in the Pisces could roughly be explained as two fishes or a fish swimming in a circular enclosure. This notwithstanding, the ministry of Jesus also had two fake twins in the persons of two brothers: Simon (Peter) and Andrew, and James and John, the sons of Zebedee.[23]

The Sun has been observed to begin its daily journey as the night passes. No place can be darker than inside of the deep cave. Hence, from the time immemorial, the Sun is deemed to be born at dawn in a cave. In the NT, the cave was changed to a manger as the dark place of birth of baby Jesus, the Sun. December 25th is also earmarked as the birthday of the past Sun (solar) deities such as Buddha, Mithras, Osiris, Horus, Hercules, Bacchus, Adonis, etc. The same was applied to the story of "Jesus Christ" by the Church. The wise men from the East who supposedly searched out and visited baby Jesus were astrologers and stargazers like the Essenes. Hence, they watched the skies for omens, including the sign of the birth of the Sun, the real saviour of the world. Without the Sun, the entire world would perish.

---

[23] Matthew 10:2

Chapter Three

MORE MEMORIES OF THE SERPENT

During the Ten Plagues in Egypt, the supernatural transformation of a stick to the serpent was one high-point of the contest.[24] Ironically Moses in the "wilderness" made a bronze serpent, which saved the Israelites from death after a fiery serpent attack.[25] That very serpent effigy was to become an idol worshipped by the Israelites at a later time.[26] Nowadays, the serpent on a winged tree/stick is a symbol of medicine and pharmaceutical services. This is often referred to as the rod of Asclepius or Caduceus, a staff carried by Hermes in Greek mythology. The 'serpent and stick' story was long in existence before the emergence of the Greeks. Hence, the idea was copied from somewhere.

In the Book of Isaiah, mention is made about "the flying serpent."[27] The question is, 'who has ever heard of a serpent that flies'? However, since the Bible mentions it, it is necessary to consider some likelihood and check references from the other lands. Outside the Bible, the only culture that celebrates "the plumed serpent" or "the winged serpent" is the Mayan people of Mesoamerica. Incidentally, they have a unique calendar that has a span of 144,000 days. The calendar is called B'ak'tun in the Long Count Calendar.

Is it a coincidence that the book of Revelation in the Bible also mentions that only 144,000 souls shall be saved from among the Israelites, followed by multitudes from all

---

[24] Exodus 7
[25] Numbers 21
[26] 2 King 18:4
[27] Isaiah 14:29; 30:6

other nations and tribes? Is the use of the exact figure of 144,000 in the Bible a pointer to a common origin and secret romance with the Mayan calendar? More interesting is the fact that the Mayan Long Count Calendar has a start-up date of 3113 BCE. This was a very long time before the nation of Israel came into existence. Hence, the Mayan calendar has much older antiquity than the Israelites, the Jews, and the Torah.

The information gathered about the Mayan plumed serpent is that between 3,500 – 3,100 BCE, during the last phase just before the First Egyptian Dynasty emerged, there was great unrest over Egypt for about 350 years following strive among the Egyptian chieftains (gods). Zechariah Sitchin[28] attributed the sudden death of Dumuzi (biblical Tammuz) to this time. This was also a time of struggle between Ra (Marduk) and his younger brother, Thoth. Following the prolonged unrest, the gods decided to withdraw from direct rule over humankind. In Egypt, at about 3100, the first human king (Pharaoh) was installed to begin the First Dynasty. According to the Greek historian, Herodotus,[29] King Mene or Men was the Pharaoh's name.

To quell the scuffle for power, Thoth abdicated the throne for his elder brother, Ra, and took some African chiefs to establish a new civilisation in the Mesoamerican region. Does this provide an answer to why there are stone heads with African features scattered in Southern America? The Egyptian god, Thoth, became a new god known as Quetzalcoatl (the winged serpent). In the ancient Sumerian clay tablets, Thoth was called Ningishzidda long before Africa was allotted to his family as an inheritance by the great god and "Father in heaven," King Anu.[30]

---

[28] See Tunji Adeeko: THEY LIED TO US

[29] Ibid.

[30] References from Zachariah Sitchin writings. See Tunji Adeeko: THEY LIED TO US – Unveiling How Christianity And Islam Religions Were Forged, chapter 12, titled "Let Us Create Man in Our Image"

In the Bible, the dragon was used interchangeably with the serpent as the symbol of Satan, the Devil.[31] In contrast to the dragon and serpent, a woman was given two wings of a GREAT EAGLE. From the above, the gestures of the Bible writers have adequately retained the memory of the serpent throughout human history. However, more importantly, it is the subtle gesture that both the Eagle and the serpent or dragon could or do *fly*. Would the flight prowess allude to some kind of aerial fleet and ancient astronauts?

---

[31] Revelation 12: 9,14,15; 20:2

Chapter Four

WHAT DOES THE SERPENT REPRESENT?

The serpent symbolism can be found across all the continents from ancient times to the modern period. In the Samaritan copy of Genesis, instead of interpreting *nachash* as "a serpent," it reads *nachash* as "a liar or deceiver," denoting a trickster. This was very much in line with the role of Satan in the Book of Job. Ironically, this is how Satan is often understood in some African folklores —a principal deity and a sacred 'messenger' or a prince among the hierarchy of the supreme beings. The Yoruba people call a deity that could roughly be identified as Satan, "Eshu."

According to late Zechariah Sitchin, who authors many books under THE EARTH CHRONICLES series and others, "the biblical term for "Serpent" literally means *Nahash,* which does not mean "snake" but the word having come from the root NHSH means "to decipher, to find out." *Nahash* could, therefore, mean "he who can decipher, he who finds things out," which perfectly depicts Enki - the chief scientist of the Anunnaki, the God of knowledge of the Nephilim. Ancient texts represent Enki with a serpent symbol, and sometimes, a double-helical serpent, most probably denoting the DNA strands.[32] I, therefore, added as a comment in my book THEY LIED TO US, that "For this reason, it has been observed over the ages, that the Seekers of Truth never fail to associate themselves with the Serpent or Dragon — the emblem of wisdom, fertility

---

[32] Zechariah Sitchin: The Wars of Gods and Men & The 12th Planet

and sexual desires. History tells us that the first secret society is the "Brotherhood of the Snake."[33]

If the Masonic signature was carefully hidden in the numerology that features 13 & 33 in the Old and New Testament, and the American Great Seal, is it also possible to detect any reference to the serpent in any modern-day document? The answer is affirmative. While discussing some bizarre features hidden in the American Dollar bill, it was observed that when the American twenty-dollar bill is folded in a particular pattern, as shown below, some hidden features are noticeable!

In figure 3 below, when lines are drawn along the folded edges, two letters can be read almost four (4) times horizontally and diagonally, "EA." EA, according to the ancient Sumerian clay tablet, is the chief deity or a prince of Nibiru. The Anunnaki made the first voyage and visited the Earth planet some 450,000 years ago, searching for a scarce mineral on their planet, GOLD. EA is pronounced 'eyah.' For his exploit, EA was given the title Enki (*En* – lord, *Ki* – earth), meaning the lord of the earth. After the flood about 13,000 years ago, which was poorly copied and wrongly dated in the Bible, Enki and his family were apportioned Africa while his younger brother. Enlil, the heir apparent, and his family were today known as Europe and Asia. Going by the symbols of the nations that settled across the globe, evidence abounds that Enki also shares in the Far East. The Enlilites were to become El among the Canaanites and later Yahweh among the Israelites and the Jews. The reason why the 'EA' in the American twenty-dollar bill may not have been connected with Enki before now is that no one seems to have previously deciphered that the scroll in the Eagle's beak stands for a serpent. More on this topic in chapter eleven.

---

[33] Tunji Adeeko: THEY LIED TO US – Unveiling How Christianity And Islam Religions Were Forged, pg 275.

FIGURE 1: AMERICAN TWENTY-DOLLAR BILL FOLDED INTO TWO

FIGURE 2: THE TWENTY-DOLLAR BILL FURTHER FOLDED AS SHOWN

FIGURE 3: LINES ARE DRAWN ALONG THE FOLDED EDGES

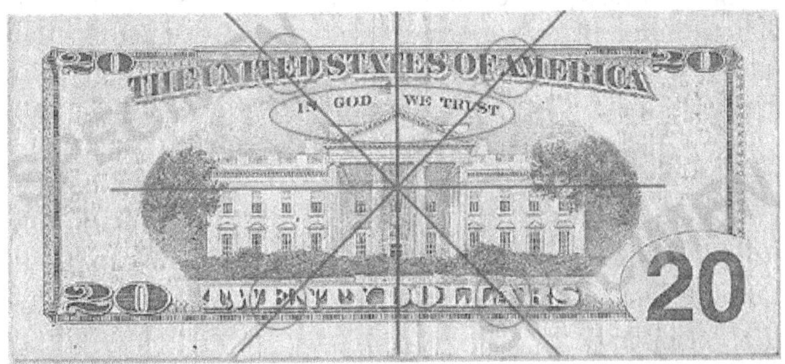

At this juncture, it is crucial if the reader of the Bible would come to terms with the fact that the creation story as it was set down is metaphorical. Following many years of archaeological expeditions which unearthed numerous ancient clay tablets at Sumer and Akkad, precisely a massive haul from the library belonging to the Assyrian King Ashurbanipal, it became necessary to reconsider what we thought we knew about the ancient past. Knowing that the date credited to the earliest clay tablets goes far back to over two and a half millennium BCE, which is a long time before the nation of Israel was born, scholars have wondered and concluded that the Bible stories are not the original version. For many reasons, it is now established that the Jewish scripture has a direct link with the characters mentioned in the unearthed ancient texts, such as Gilgamesh. The character called "Noah" in the Bible was known as Ziusudra (Sumerian) or Utnapishtim (Akkadian). The names of the Jewish months have also been identified to have origin traceable to Sumer. In these regards, it is only reasonable to admit the obvious that the Jewish scripture does not have the bragging right of a unique source for the stories and events they 'copied and shared' in the supposed holy book. The Jews adopted and refined many ancient stories, including those of Egyptian origin, without admitting who first owned the account. The act is not a mere case of theft but forgery. In light of what we now know, the Jews did not invent one-God (monotheism). The Sumerian chief deity did it for the Jews to rule the Age of Pisces [140 – 2300 CE]. Just as the Egyptian god, Ra, who became Marduk in Babylon, invented henotheism for humankind during the Age of Aries [2020 BCE – 140 CE].

Based on extracts from the Bible and other sources, the followings are the attributes of the 'serpent.'

1. The serpent of the Bible is very wise and capable of trickery acts.

2. With the multiple meanings for the Hebrew word, el-o-heem', the writer(s) of the Jewish scripture attest to the prevailing notion in the ancient world that multiple persons (gods or divine beings) were involved in the creation episode. And, most likely is the fact that the personality called 'serpent' in the Bible is one of them.

3. The serpent of the Bible is not an animal but is known by the serpent symbol. The symbol (two intertwined snakes) is believed to have been derived from the double-helical of the DNA. Hence, the person behind the serpent symbol is a great scientist, most probably a creator god.

4. Considering that there are Eagle and Serpent lineages of the 'gods and goddesses,' it is no longer a secret that the Eagle family composed and compiled the books in the Bible (see THEY LIED TO US). They, in turn, demonised the Serpent family so that the future humankind would detest whatever they stood for in Egypt and Babylon – a careful brainwash.

5. The serpent of the Bible is closely associated with astrology; he and his family most probably invented it.

6. The secret society known as the Brotherhood of the snake was most probably formed to secretly share the serpent sacred teachings among the illuminated ones (Illuminati), the Freemasons, and other secret societies.

7. References to 'a flying serpent' or dragon or a woman with the wing of a great eagle secretly allude the persons behind the serpent and eagle masks as those capable of controlling fleets of flying machines. This should open an inquiry into the

incidence of the flying saucers, UFOs, or ancient astronaut's theory.

Figure 4: CADUCEUS

8. When we carefully consider the Caduceus (Figure 4), that is, the two snakes entwined around a winged stick, it reveals that the two most significant objects of reference given to humanity are the SERPENT & EAGLE symbols.

9. The serpent's name, as inscribed in the American $20 bill, is "EA." Ea was Enki in the Akkadian language, Ptah, in Egypt. One of the meanings of the name 'Egypt' comes from the ancient term Hutkaptah, meaning 'temple of the soul of Ptah.'[34] In Greece, Ea became known as Neptune and Poseidon in Rome. The serpent's brother Enlil became "EL" among the Canaanites and later the Israelites. Enlil has the Eagle epithet and became Zeus in Greece and Jupiter in Rome.

---

[34] Histories of Nations – How their identities were forged. Published by Thames & Hudson, pg 15.

Chapter Five

THE JEWISH CREATION DATE

It is puzzling how the Jewish scripture and calendar have been used to indoctrinate the world falsely. Subliminally, the Jewish scripture and its chronology claim that "God" created the world or the earth and humankind very recently, that is, 3,761 or 3,760 BCE. The Jewish or Hebrew Masoretic calendar recognises this year 2020 CE as A.M. 5,780 (AM or A.M. is derived from the Latin words Anno Mundi[35] meaning "in the year of the world" - Year After Creation). The Greek Septuagint text was in use till the 6th century, which has a disparity of about 1,749 years from the date set in the former. I believe that the discrepancy in the Septuagint was intentionally created for a reason stated below.

The change in the calendar from the Greek Septuagint to the Hebrew Masoretic calendar was necessitated due to the former calendar hitting the 6,000-year-old mark (AM 6,000) from the creation of Adam, indicating a possible end of the world anytime in the 6th century. The change in the calendar by a Catholic monk known as Dionysus Exiguus or Denis the Little, therefore, became an exigency. It involved using the two different dates alluded to as the birth dates of Jesus Christ to arrive at year 1 (1 CE or AD 1). AD or A.D. is sometimes erroneously read as "After the Death" instead of a short for the Latin phrase "*Anno Domini*" – 'in the year of the Lord. Or, from the birth of Jesus Christ.

As already pointed out in chapter one and unknown to many Christians, in the book of Matthew, the date for the birth of Jesus was set at 6 BCE while Luke carefully put

---

[35] https://en.wikipedia.org/wiki/Anno_Mundi

45

the birth of Jesus at Caesar Augustus' census that took place AD 7 (7 CE). Naturally, the Bible readers' minds were never trained to detect the apparent disparity. If they do, some will attribute it to a possible error by Luke, while others would argue and waive the contradiction aside as not so important to cause any damage to the Gospel. The admittance of any mistake from Luke is sufficient to question the authenticity and reliability of the New Testament as a book inspired by God. However, to a monk such as Denis, this was no mistake but a purposefully written record. It was a secret code, set up in advance, by those who anticipated and planned the change in the calendar. Hence, for the first time in human history, a calendar was concocted and registered by the Church as "*Anno Domini* nostri Jesu Christi DXXXII) or AD 532, meaning "in the year of our Lord (Jesus Christ) 532."

Furthermore, unknown to the Bible readers, by the careful adoption of AD 1 in the 6th century as the birth year of Jesus Christ, the Church has ingeniously made possible the fulfillment of another prophecy in the Book of Daniel. I discussed this topic extensively in chapter eighteen of my book THEY LIED TO US, titled *The 2300 Days of Daniel Finally Decoded.*

"Zodiac," according to Encarta, is the constellation of stars found on the apparent path of the Sun. The Sun's path occupies an "imaginary belt in the celestial sphere. The pathway extends for about 8° on either side of the ecliptic. The width of the zodiac was initially determined to include the orbits of the Sun and Moon and of the five planets (Mercury, Venus, Mars, Jupiter, and Saturn) that were known to the people of ancient times. They divided the zodiac into 12 sections of 30° each, which are called the signs of the zodiac. Starting from the vernal equinox and then proceeding eastward along the ecliptic, each of the divisions is named for the constellation situated within its limits in the 2nd century BCE. The names of the zodiacal signs are Aries, the Ram; Taurus, the Bull; Gemini, the

Twins; Cancer, the Crab; Leo, the Lion; Virgo, the Virgin; Libra, the Balance; Scorpio, the Scorpion; Sagittarius, the Archer; Capricorn, the Goat; Aquarius, the Water Bearer; and Pisces, the Fishes.

Following the right decode of Daniel 8:14 concerning the prophecy of 2300 days of Daniel, the motive of the Bible writer is now self-evident. While the Bible writers believed in astrology as a natural guardian of events on earth, the introduction of the Anno Domini was intended to throw any researcher off course. It is not surprising that some scholars would naturally imagine that the Age of Pisces commenced with the birth of Jesus Christ in A.D. 1. This is not true, but it was intentionally recorded to mislead those who would not know what to find.

Despite the false lead by the Bible authors, it is clear that every effort was still made to ensure that the correct counting of the astrological age is never lost. Not lost to those who would crack the code, just as the author of this book has rightly done. With the proper alignment of the Gregorian calendar alongside the astrological age, human history can now be established to have undergone the following period. Please, bear in mind that 'age' is recognised to span an approximate 2,160 years, with an adjustable margin of ±6 years.) The reader will also note that I have slightly deviated from the Zechariah Sitchin reckoning of the Age dates. I made the corrections based on the authority of the Bible writers, whom, I presume, have superior knowledge.

Age of Taurus (the Bull):	*4180 – 2020 BCE*
Age of Aries (the Ram):	*2020 BCE – 140 CE*
Age of Pisces (the Fishes):	*140 – 2300 CE*
Age of Aquarius (Water-bearer):	*2300 – 4460 CE*

*   *   *

There is a scientific research popularly term 'the Mitochondria Eve."[36] It pitched the origin of modern man, Homo sapiens, between 315,000 – 180,000 years ago. This finding, no doubt, negates Adam's chronology, which stated 3,760 BCE. Ironically, recent archaeology findings have thrown up an ancient settlement in Israel regions dated 9,000 years ago.[37] Archaeology works have also unearthed pots and pot sheds in Sudan dated to 10,000 BCE. How do we reconcile this with the 3,760 BCE creation date for Adam and Eve?

In 1965, an English archaeologist, late Prof Thurstan Shaw, and his team hired a helicopter to make a historic visit to the thick forest of Isarun. Traditionally, this place is called Isarun Ile-Owuro, (Isarun the ancient land), a sleepy village in Ondo State, Southwestern Nigeria, about 20 kilometres to Akure, five kilometres to Igbara Oke. They worked rigorously and excavated bones of Stone Age man. The skeleton was confirmed as dating to about 13,000 years ago. However, the skull did not look like one from a recent human, particularly those living in West Africa today. Instead, it shared many similarities with African fossil skulls that date to more than 100,000 years ago. It is longer and flatter with a strong brow ridge. It has features closer to a much older skull from Tanzania, thought to be around 140,000 years old. This discovery is no doubt another puncture to the Jewish 3,760 BCE creation date.

Bishop Ussher, having studied the Bible, submitted that the world was created in the early morning of 4004 BCE, completed alongside the creation of Adam. It is near impossible to extract any date beyond 4,000 BCE from the chronology in the Hebrew scripture except where the corrupted Septuagint is used. When the ancient world is revisited and thoroughly probed with copious dateable and

---

[36] https://en.wikipedia.org/wiki/Mitochondrial_Eve
[37] https://www.bbc.com/news/world-middle-east-49002046

measurable materials unearthed, it is glaringly that the stories in the Holy Books are found wanting in many areas.

With the 100,000 – 140,000-year-old skeleton found in my backyard in Africa, it will be foolish of me as a black man to go on believing that God created the first human in Mesopotamia circa 3,760 BCE. If this claim persists, it then means that the Africans and perhaps other coloured races are Pre-Adamite. And if this should be the case, then the sin committed by Adam and Eve should never be visited upon the black race and other Pre-Adamite races. Hence, the story of Jesus was blatantly lied told to enslave the African minds and the world. The claim by the theologians that one day is with the Lord as a thousand years and a thousand years as one day[38] is a fraudulent statement. The statement cannot and should not be applied to Biblical stories; else, there would be the need to review the same Bible contents. The Age of Methuselah would possibly come to 969,000 years or approximately one million years old when he died. From all indications, the more one looks into the Bible; the more one is faced with a stark reality that the book is indeed a *pious fraud* put together by society like the Masonic society or the Illuminati of old to control human souls.

---

[38] 2 Peter 3:8

Chapter Six

THE JEWS AND THE SUMERIAN TEXTS

From Zechariah Sitchin's interpretation of the Sumerian clay tablets and archaeology findings, the date 3,800 – 3,760 BCE was a Nibiru Window. In order words, the abode of extraterrestrial visitors, the Nibiru planet (either a real or artificial planetary object in space, as some have lately argued) spends about 40 years within the Earth space in its 3,600 years elliptical orbit around our sun. According to many ancient texts such as the Sumerian, Babylonian, and even the Bible, the inhabitants of Nibiru and possibly other beings from other planets have had intercourse with earth from time immemorial before the emergence of life and human civilisation. And this will account mainly for the many out-of-place-artefacts found in awkward places across the globe for which there is no human history to explain the phenomenon.

Long before the first dynasty period in Mesopotamia and Egypt, the "gods" or extraterrestrial being or scions from the long lost civilisations of Atlantis, Lemuria, and perhaps others rarely mentioned were visiting and roaming the earth. The near recent period of Age of Leo, the Lion, 10,660 - 8,150 BCE produced the Sphinx, "a stone structure primarily carved out of solid limestone bedrock, with parts of its legs and outer body encased in limestone blocks. The 66 feet tall at the head is 240 feet long with a lion's body and the head of a man." The original Sphinx was thought to have been with a lion or lioness' head. It is also believed that the current human head on the Sphinx was re-carved from the first head at a later time. This will explain why the current head is very small in proportion to the much larger body. The Sphinx is a very laudable hallmark of prehistoric Egypt.

I am aware that some Egyptologists, who though are not geologists, would argue for a date of about 2,500 BCE for the construction of the Sphinx. However, some authorities have studied the vertical weathering patterns on the Sphinx. In addition to the small human head, they submitted that the weathering could only have been caused by rainfall thousands of years before that region became a Sahara desert. A reference report was made by the Boston University geologist Robert Schoch in 1991. He based his conclusions on the extensive weathering caused by rainfall, which is not found on the pyramids or any other monuments on the Giza plain. Another discovery is the Göbekli Tepe with the world's oldest known megaliths in Turkey, dated to 10,0000 BCE. If this is true, why could the Sphinx not have been built between 10,000 – 8,000 BCE?

The Bible largely contradicts the ancient world-views that the gods and goddesses of old, possibly the ancient astronauts, were anthropomorphic. "They were as physically similar to mortal men and women, and human in character. They could be happy and angry and jealous; they made love, quarrelled, fought, and they procreated like humans – bringing forth offspring through sexual intercourse - with each other or with humans. They were unreachable, and yet constantly mixed up in human affairs. They could travel at immense speeds, appear and disappear; they had weapons of immense and unusual power."

Why would the Bible explicitly deny enormous antiquity for the age of the earth and human beings on earth? The answer is straightforward: the extraterrestrial beings who groomed the earth as their colony would prefer to hide their identity from humankind. Besides, when a faction of the olden deities chose to rule the Age of Pisces using the Caucasians post-exilic period, they remolded human history and limited human attention to the dynastic era of Mesopotamia and Egypt when civilisation was granted to humankind.

Marduk, during the Babylonia era and in the Age of Aries [2020 BCE – 140CE], shifted human attention from many other deities of Mesopotamia, unto himself and his son, Nabu. It is of no surprise, therefore, that when Enlil's lineage adopted the Jews from Babylonia 'heresy,' they also formulate an advanced religious philosophy where the symbol of Enki, the serpent, was set as the enmity of humanity, Satan. They also reformulated a religious ideology which contrasted the memory of the many deities of old into a mono (one) theism (God), possibly borrowed from the existence of the lone Sun.

In Enûma Eliš, the Babylonia Epic of Creation, the accidental collision of Nibiru's moons with the primaeval Tiamat (a giant planet covered with water) was said to have resulted in the creation of the Earth. This contact is assumed to have seeded life to the resulting new planet. The earth, after that, developed via evolution processes. Thus, it is concluded that the origin of life goes far beyond the era when the primaeval Tiamat was pierced and divided to become Earth, billions of years ago.

This idea was subtly subscribed to by the Bible writers when it is written saying:

> *In the beginning God created the heaven and*
> *the earth. And the earth was without form,*
> *and void; and darkness was upon the face of*
> *the deep. And the Spirit of God moved upon*
> *the face of the waters.*[39]

Modern awareness affirms that there are more than a trillion planets in the universe. Therefore, from the above passage, there is the need to redefine the meaning of "in the beginning." If the Bible writer had restricted "the

---

[39] Genesis 1:1-2

beginning" to 3,760 BCE of the Bible chronology, starting from the creation of Adam and Eve in the Garden of Eden, somewhere in Mesopotamia, then this is a big fraud. The story as presently lay down in the Torah, and the Bible is a fraud. The Biblical account of creation is a myth. The Garden of Eden is a myth. The story that Adam and Eve were the first human couple on the earth planet who gave birth to all human populations within the last 6,000 years is a myth. Many of the stories that found their ways into the Bible were borrowed from many ancient sources.[40] If anyone would make an argument for the Jews, first, let the Jews tell the world the meaning of 3,760 BCE in their calendar.

In the light of what is today known about the antiquity of human history, modern Christians and Muslims cannot continue to play the ostrich. The Jewish scripture was never inspired but fabricated by the Sumerian gods and their Elite accomplice. The same is true about the Qur'an. Before the coming of the Prophet, the Arabs were idol worshippers like many ancient societies. All the prophets mentioned in the Qur'an are those preserved in the Jewish Scripture. Therefore, if any statement is credited to any ancient prophet and such is not directly inferred from the Jewish holy books, it is essential to query how such statements were preserved for Prophet Mohammed and his followers. It is absurd to accept that GOD wrote the biographies of the dead patriarchs and separately kept them in the book we now call Qur'an. Christianity and Islam are two sides of the same coin; the coin was minted by the many ancient deities who later assumed the One-God status to hide their true identity.

This was the hidden Babylonia Agenda, which I made open in the book THEY LIED TO US. I put forward in detail how, when, why, and what the Sumerian god, Enlil, did to thwart the Age of Aries from the hand of Marduk/Ra

---

[40] See chapter 7 of THEY LIED TO US titled The Sources of The Stories In The Bible.

after the Jews (a then heavily coloured race) was released from the Babylonia Captivity. For the reason that is not so clear, the Nibiru Council decided to use Rome and the Romans to rule the Age of Pisces. The rejection of the Jewish people and the land of Israel had nothing to do with the killing of a fictitious messiah because such a thing never happened in the first century.

From all known facts, it was the Roman elites who worked under the pen name of Flavius Josephus, the so-called first-century *Jewish* historian and others such as Pliny and Proculus, to create a new religion to drown Judaism. From this background, it is, therefore, no hidden secret that the Vatican used the same Jesus Christ storyline to create Islam in the sixth and seventh centuries. We know how the Vatican created Islam from the revelations shared by an ex-Jesuit late Dr Rivera Alberto. This revelation and many others help researchers to recognise that the two religions of Christianity and Islam are the brainchild of the Anunnaki brothers. The myth of a virgin-born prophet is the heart of the two religions – a storyline that runs parallel with the story of Horus, an ancient Egyptian god, and perhaps that of Krishna of India also.

The story of Adam and Eve in Mesopotamia is the Sumerian gods' leash on the Jews. It is a tag that the Jews cannot remove. Else, they would openly admit that the monotheism that was invented for them was forged.

Chapter Seven

A REVIEW OF HUMAN HISTORY USING FOUR CALENDARS

I reviewed human history by interposing three ancient calendars on the Gregorian calendar. See Figure 5 on page 58. These are:

1. The Nibiru Orbit makes a 3,600 years elliptical movement around our sun according to the ancient Sumerian text, as translated by the late Zachariah Sitchin.

2. The astrological age: The Babylonians recognised that 12 zodiac constellations exist within the "imaginary belt in the celestial sphere, extending about 8° on either side of the ecliptic, the apparent path of the Sun among the stars." The astrologers identify that in approximately 2,160 years (±6 years), the sun passes each zodiac constellation. One Great Year equals 25,920 years of precession when the sun must have passed through all the constellations.

3. The Maya Long Count calendar has a b'ak'tun of 144,000 days.

4. The Gregorian calendar: 365 days make a year, and 366 days make a leap year.

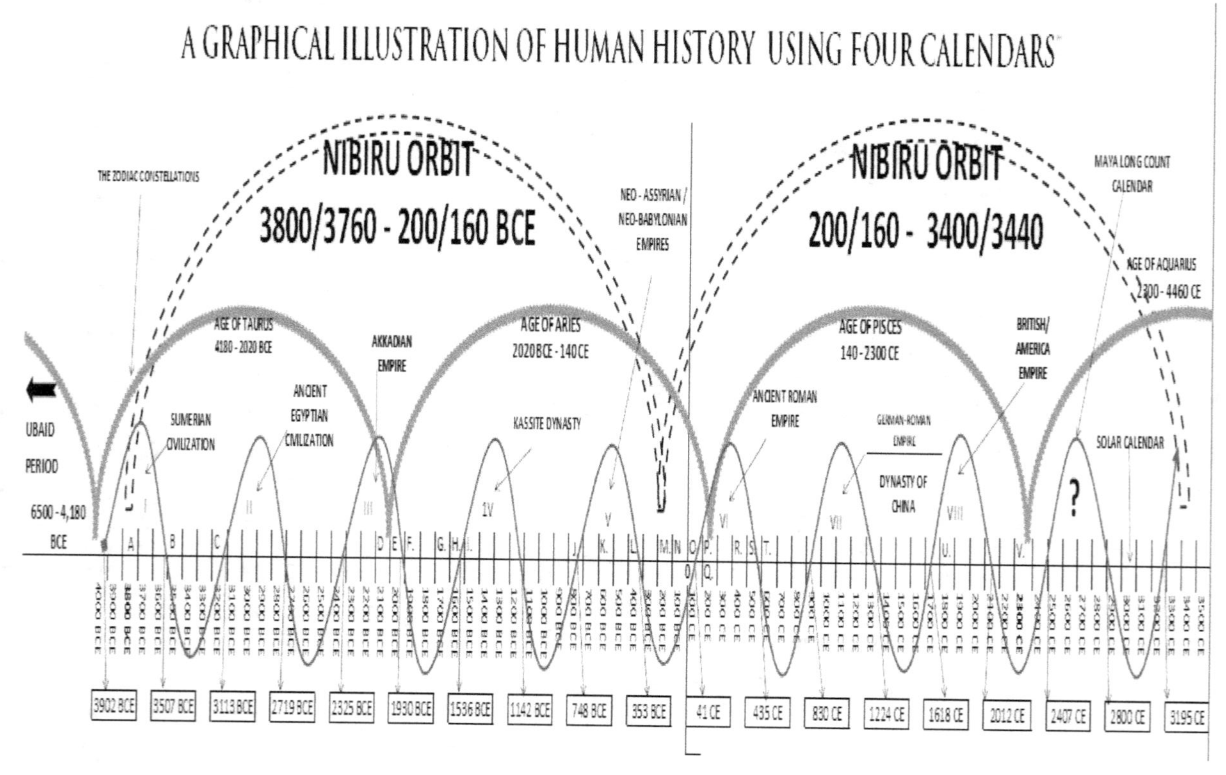

A GRAPHICAL ILLUSTRATION OF HUMAN HISTORY USING FOUR CALENDARS
THE ZODIAC CONSTELLATIONS
NIBIRU ORBIT 3800/3760 - 200/160 BCE
NEO - ASSYRIAN / NEO-BABYLONIAN EMPIRES
NIBIRU ORBIT 200/160 - 3400/3440
MAYA LONG COUNT CALENDAR
AGE OF TAURUS 4180 - 2020 BCE
AKKADIAN EMPIRE
AGE OF ARIES 2020 BCE - 140 CE
AGE OF PISCES 140 - 2300 CE
BRITISH/ AMERICA EMPIRE
AGE OF AQUARIUS 2300 - 4460 CE
UBAID PERIOD 6500 - 4,180 BCE
SUMERIAN CIVILIZATION
ANCIENT EGYPTIAN CIVILIZATION
KASSITE DYNASTY
ANCIENT ROMAN EMPIRE
GERMAN-ROMAN EMPIRE
DYNASTY OF CHINA
SOLAR CALENDAR
?
3902 BCE
3507 BCE
3113 BCE
2719 BCE
2325 BCE
1930 BCE
1536 BCE
1142 BCE
748 BCE
353 BCE
41 CE
435 CE
830 CE
1224 CE
1618 CE
2012 CE
2407 CE
2800 CE
3195 CE

The reader will observe that the Jewish creation myth of Adam and Eve, which was recorded as an event that took place in 3,760 BCE, is conspicuously displayed at the far left on the diagram. Wikipedia puts the Ubaid period at 6,500 – 3,800 BCE. The foundation of the first temple of Enki, post the Deluge, was made in Eridu circa 3,800 BCE. Subsequently, the Jewish calendar, designed at the temple of Enlil at Nippur,[41] has a starting date of 3,760 BCE. Therefore, 3,800 – 3,760 BCE was a Nibiru Window.

On the far right on the diagram, the 2300 days of Daniel [Daniel 8:14] represents the termination year for the Age of Pisces [140 – 2,300 CE.]. The graphical illustration, therefore, represents the totality of a worldview as contained in the Hebrew scripture. This is the summary of the Sumerian brainwash. According to the Bible, no world existed before 3,760 BCE since Yahweh Elohim (LORD God) created Adam and Eve in that year – this is a big lie. This worldview does not in any way represent the real human history where monuments of great antiquity littered the prehistoric world. Hence, one can conclude that the Bible writers intend to constrain and control the information given to the human race using the organised religions of Judaism, Christianity, and Islam.

To believe in the Biblical stories and the controlled worldview is to accept that humankind is still in the slave camp of the Sumerian deities. The Jews, the Arabs, and the West are their chief propagandists. It is not surprising. Therefore, the nations who are steep deep in religious indoctrinations barely explores the universe. That is the job for GOD, the Anunnaki gods, The mind of the leaders and citizens of the third world countries are greatly veiled. These nations barely make any breakthrough in technological advancements.

America and European nations are different though they are also people of the Christian faith. They, in

---

[41] See THEY LIED TO US

particular, know the GOD they serve as the Sumerian deities, which aid them in the transfer of technology and other space knowledge. The Russians, Chinese, Japanese, and other nations knew these truths that no Yahweh Elohim created any Adam and Eve in Mesopotamia. Despite their dislike of religion as defined by the West, they are recognised as great nations. Russian and some European countries are significantly related to the West, and as we shall soon find out, they share a common symbol – the Eagle and double headed-Eagle.

The third world countries have no clue, but continuously they await a saviour that never was and would never come back. They grab lands and destroy farmland with the use of terrorists and cattle rustlers. They fight senseless wars called Holy Jihad and grope in the darkness of eternal ignorance and self-inflicted terrorism. The game players use them as pawns, ever consuming, and producing nothing. They imagined that the senseless killing, the enshrined illiteracy, poverty, and biological expansion of the religious population through uncontrolled childbirth is service to GOD. The masses and the elites have been deceived for centuries, and the earlier they wake up from this deep slumber, the better for them.

A. THE UBAID PERIOD

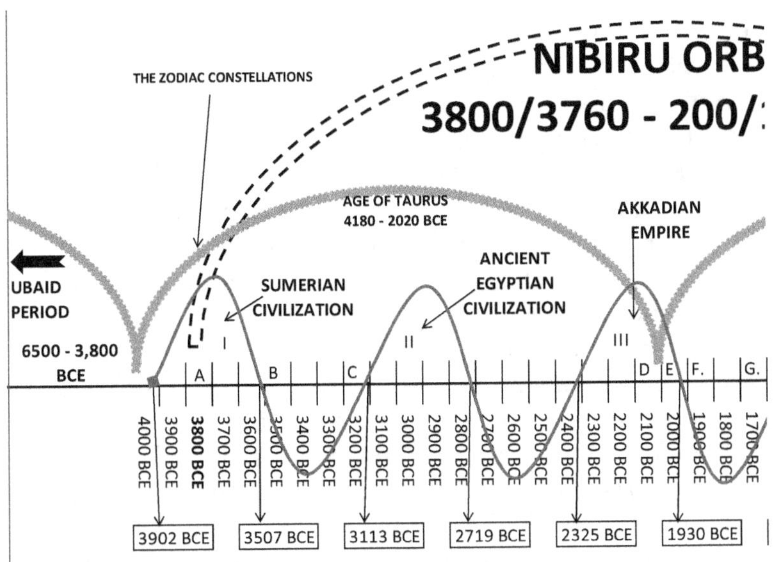

UBAID PERIOD: The black arrow on the left edge of the diagram points to the Ubaid Period of 6,500 – 3,800 BCE, according to Wikipedia. It makes almost an overlapping period with the Age of Gemini of 6,340 – 4,180 BCE. Evidence of human settlements was excavated in Mesopotamia during the Ubaid period. The settlement had an inferior civilisation when compared with that of Sumer. The people of that period are referred to as the Lizard people. In contrast, the Sumerian civilisation has *recorded* the "first" of so many achievements in human history.[42]

---

[42]See Samuel Noah Kramer's book – History Begins At Sumer.

B. THE AGE OF TAURUS

The Age of Taurus fell on 4,180 – 2,020 BCE (±6 years).
It is pertinent to note that this age started with Sumerian (human) civilisation in Mesopotamia and spread to the Ancient Egyptian (human) civilisation in Africa and later the Akkadian Empire. The last empire covered Mesopotamia and reached the Far East (Russia, India, Japan, and China). According to the ancient text, Enlil was the head of the Sumerian pantheon while Ea/Enki/Ptah was the head of the Egyptian pantheon. The Akkadian Empire was ruled by a goddess, the grand-daughter of Enlil – Inanna/Ishtar, who first married Dumuzi, the biblical Tammuz. Still, the marriage did not produce any child before Dumuzi mysteriously died.[43] Ishtar later married Sargon the Great or Sargon of Agade. There were overlapping and collaborative activities among the deities, and there were strives also. This era witnessed **polytheism,** and different people freely worship the god or goddess in their domains.

---

[43] The unfruitful but highly celebrated marriage between the god and goddess, Dumuzi and Inanna, has been preserved in a Christian religious festival. The ancient practice known as the weeping for Dumuzi or Tammuz has become the observation of Good Friday preceding the celebration of the resurrection of a supposed Jesus Christ on the Easter Festival. In truth, this is a festival in honour of the goddess of fertility –Ishtar or Innana. The Christian popular annual festivals of a Good Friday and Easter, have nothing to do with the death and resurrection of Jesus Christ. A careful review of the supposed life of Jesus Christ in the Bible reveals that the records are inconsistent; hence, the record was fabricated. See Resurrection Episode Revisited on pages 178 – 181, THEY LIED TO US – Unveiling How Christianity and Islam Religions Were Forged

C. THE AGE OF ARIES

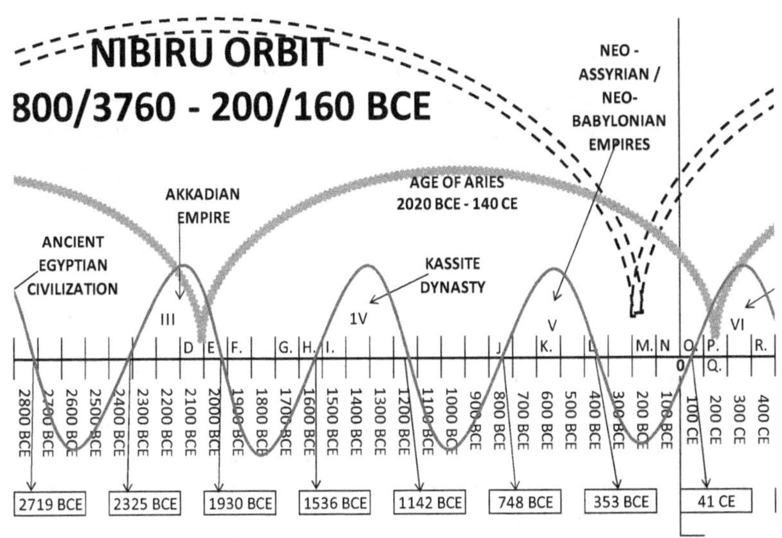

The Age of Aries fell on the years 2,020 BCE – 140 CE (±6 years)

In the early days of the New Age, King Hammurabi was a significant ruler, and the stele of Hammurabi recognises Marduk (the first son of Ea/Enki/Ptah but otherwise known as Ra or Amen-Ra in Egypt) as the god who granted Hammurabi the kingship over the Kassites and Babylon. During this Age, the Enûma Eliš[44] or Babylonia creation story was the primary tool for religious indoctrination. The idea was to promote Marduk and his son, Nabu, as the central and supreme gods. All other deities in the old Sumer and Akkad were relegated to the

---

[44] https://www.ancient.eu/article/225/enuma-elish---the-babylonian-epic-of-creation---fu/

background, and their shrines were restricted to remote villages except for few goddesses. In the major cities, Marduk and Nabu were chief deities. The name of King Nebuchadnezzar of Babylon means *"O god Nabu, protect/preserve my first son."*

When the Assyrians overran Babylon, they continued with Enûma Eliš but changed the name of Marduk to Ashur. Ashur or Assur was the capital of Assyria. It is, therefore, essential to note that the Enûma Eliš in its original form, where Nibiru 'battled' Tiamat is not a myth but an ancient cosmogony that was set down in the best language possible. However, the story became a myth or a legend when Enlil, Marduk, and Ashur were substituted for Nibiru. During the Age of Aries, religious practice was **henotheism** – the worship of one god (Marduk with his son, Nabu) while acknowledging other (Anunnaki) deities. It is reported in history that the Babylonian Akitu Festival[45] was observed deep into the ancient Roman Empire period. This was an annual festival in the honour of Marduk and Nabu throughout the Babylonia Empire.

The Jews, up till the Babylonia captivity, were practising **monolatry** (the worship of only one god without, however, denying the existence of other gods). Hence, Enlil (El) turned Yahweh was only one god among other Canaanite gods and goddesses. In 2005, the Syro-Palestinian Professor Emeritus of Near Eastern Archaeology and Anthropology at the University of Arizona, William G. Dever, published a book titled: Did God Have a Wife? The book was about archaeological findings, which indicated that Yahweh was thought to have a wife, Ashtoreth. Ashtoreth is otherwise known as Ishtar or Inaana.

For those who are familiar with the historical return of the Jews from the Babylonia Captivity, one can identify on the illustration above that 538 BCE downwards fell just

---

[45] https://en.wikipedia.org/wiki/Akitu

before the last interregnum (353 BCE – 41 CE) when the Age of Aries was to give way to the New Age (of Pisces). This was the period in the 6th century when the religion of the One-God called **monotheism** was invented.

D. THE AGE OF PISCES

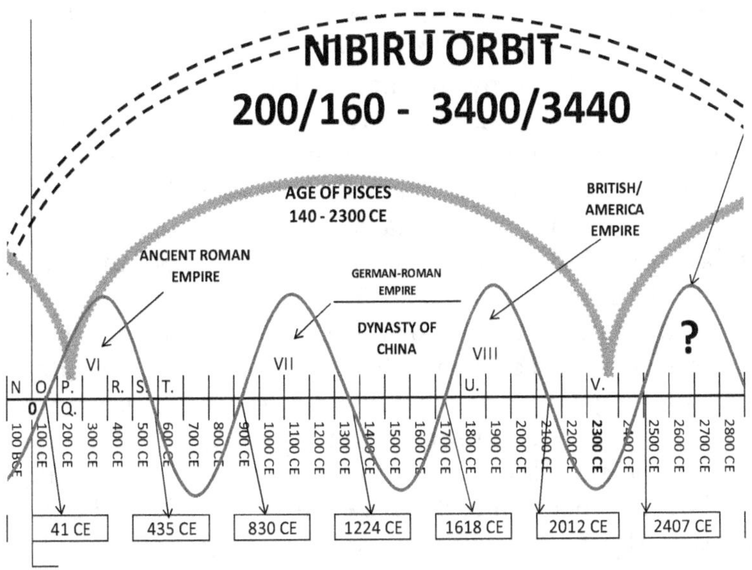

The Age of Pisces started from 140 CE and extended to the current period. This Age commenced with the exploits of the ancient Roman Empire, which transformed into becoming the German-Roman Empire and, lastly, into the British-America Empire.

Starting from the Jewish creation story, which stipulates 3,760 BCE as the date for creating the first human race on earth, it is now clear that this is a mere fallacy and forgery. This date was flagged to commemorate when the Anunnaki lords granted civilisation to the humankind, post the Deluge, at Sumer during the Nibiru

Window of 3,800 – 3,760 BCE. The world was never created at about 3,760 BCE. The first couple was never created on this date except that the story peddled in the Bible is referring to the further genetic manipulation of the existing archaic humans of the Denisovan, Neandertal man, and lately, the black race or an alien species to produce the white race (Caucasians). Mesopotamia was never the cradle of Homo sapiens but Africa. The chief scientist (creator) and the central brain behind the upgrade of the DNA of apes to that of the intelligent human, as recorded in the ancient Sumerian and Akkadian texts as translated by the late Zechariah Sitchin and many others, was Ea/Enki/Ptah. He worked in the company of other female scientists, including Ninhursag. They researched in Africa. It has also been established that first modern Britons were "dark to black" skinned.[46] The emigration of Homo sapiens from Africa was put at 80,000 – 100,000 years ago.

An excellent review of the past two thousand years of human history confirms that the memory and glory of ancient Egypt and Babylon were carefully suppressed. The Bible was primarily used to demonised the serpent symbol of the ancient Egyptian pharaohs. In the same vein, the Jewish holy book and the New Testament have been used to steal the human future by promoting that a "Messiah the Prince" is coming back the second time when, from all indications, there was never a historical person called Jesus the Christ in the first century. There is no ground to expect any Return.

---

[46] https://www.theguardian.com/science/2018/feb/07/first-modern-britons-dark-black-skin-cheddar-man-dna-analysis-reveals

E. WHO RULED THE AGES?

AGE OF TAURUS (4,180 – 2,020 BCE)

All the chief deities in their respective abodes ruled the age. Enlil was the head of the pantheon in Sumer, and he led from Nippur. Enki was the head of the pantheon in Egypt though he came from Eridu of Mesopotamia. Inaana or Ishtar was the head of the pantheon in Akkad. People in different lands adopted religions of their choice. The religious ideology was **Polytheism,** which degenerated into pantheism in India and the worship of ancestors (who originally could have been aliens) in China and other regions.

AGE OF ARIES (2,020 BCE – 140 CE)

The serpent family ruled the age with Marduk leading the family. He chose to rule from Babylon because it was one of the earliest settlements established by his father, Enki. The first city founded by Enki is Eridu, and it is today known as the world's oldest city.[47] According to the Sumerian scribes, Eridu is regarded as the oldest settlement in the world, where "kingship first came from heaven." In Egypt, Marduk, in absentia, became Ra, the 'hidden' or 'unseen' god. The nations under the Enlil's family's control made incursions and attempted to snatch many lands from the Enkites. In the last quarter of the Age, that is, from 540 BCE, the Eagle family began to push for a new religious idea, using the Jews. The main religious idea during this age was **Henotheism** in Babylon, built

---

[47] See Wikipedia

around Marduk as the principal deity, alongside his son, Nabu. According to the Cyrus cylinder, the victory of the Persian emperor over Babylon in 538 BCE was credited to Marduk's support for the new Emperor even though he was not from Babylon. In other lands, polytheism persisted across many lands.

AGE OF PISCES (140 – 2,300 CE)

The Greeks conquered the Persians. And the content of the Jewish scripture was further revised from 353 BCE to the first century by agents loyal to Enlilite's agenda. After that, the New Testament was written by the Roman aristocrats and never by the people whose names are inscribed on each book covers. The New Age copied many things from the practices of the Serpent family that ruled ancient Egypt, Babylon, Africa as a whole, and bits and pieces from the Persians and other sources. All these were mixed up to create the religious ideology that exists today as **Monotheism**.

The Romans, coming from the background of a polytheistic society inherited from the Greeks, struggled with strict monotheism in the first four or five centuries. The Synoptic Gospels were written on the premises of "Had There Been A Messiah." Characters, like a stage drama, were developed for what the Messiah would say and how he would act. However, the complex Roman religious background made the Trinity doctrine a necessity. The philosophy of Trinity abridged the real history of the ancient world and the then New Age. Rightly put, Trinity is a heavily summarized polytheism. The Sumerian pantheons were completed with the canonisation of saints, who serve as the larger family of the ancient key gods and goddesses.

As if the inventors of the one-God concept, far back in Babylon, were not happy with what the Roman turned

Christianity into, they created Islam in the seventh century as a more strict monotheism. If these were done to widen the net to caught more souls into monotheism, this act turned out to weaken the arguments on monotheistic ideology. As things are, no sane person would regard that one God harvests people through Mecca and Saudi Arabia ports into Islam and, at the time, harvest people through Rome and West ports into Christianity. The criteria for accepting people into each fold is contradictory; hence, there can never be the same hereafter for the two religious followers except in an argument for political exigencies. For those who could critically consider the scenario, it is not a matter of Christianity is better than Islam or vice versa; the two beliefs are mutually exclusive. They were both built on the faulty foundation of the Sumerian masters; hence, they are false. If there is ONE GOD, no one knows what SHE, HE, or IT looks like, and from the records provided to humankind in the holy books of the Torah, New Testament, and Qur'an, humanity has been grossly brainwashed. Hinduism, Buddhism, Christianity, Islam, Traditional beliefs, and Atheism are the proverbial six blind men who visited an elephant and called it different things based on the body part they touched.

According to the order of time as preserved in the Mayan calendar, the last phase in the Age of Pisces, the 13th b'ak'tun, was under the control of the British-American Empire. This period came to an end in the year 2012 [1618 – 2012]. In the following 14th b'ak'tun, which comprises 144,000 days or 394.25 years starting from December 21, 2012, the world shall witness possible technologically driven battles to restructure human history. For those who are willing to face reality, Christianity is already winding down its business. Ditto for Islam, they came together, and they will go down together. There was never any Jesus Christ in the first century; the calendar was carefully manipulated to tell whatever stories peddled on the subject matter.

When we use the Bible[48] further as a guide, a new dynasty or world power or a confederation of global powers will be put in place thereabout 2300 CE to rule the New Age, the AGE OF AQUARIUS. It may take another century for this new world power to break away from the old principles and style, but the emergence is sure and unwavering.

---

[48] Daniel 8:13,14

Chapter Eight

THE EVIDENCE THAT THE SERPENT ONCE RULED

FIGURE 6: PHARAOH AKHENATEN HEAD BUST

FIGURE 7: PHARAOH AMENHOTEP III HEAD BUST

FIGURE 8: PHARAOH SETI 1 AND GODDESS MAAT TEMPLE RELIEF.

FIGURE 9: PHARAOH SEN-USERET III HEAD BUST

FIGURE 10: GOLD MASK OF TUTANKHAMUN

FIGURE 11: PHARAOH AMENEMHAT HEAD BUST

FIGURE 12: PHARAOH TUTANKHAMUN HEAD BUST

FIGURE 13: PHARAOH RAMESES II HEAD BUST

Chapter Nine

THE EVIDENCE OF EAGLE FAMILY'S RULE

FIGURE 14: ANCIENT GREEK COIN

FIGURE 15: ANCIENT ROMAN COIN

FIGURE 16: ROMAN EAGLE PENDANT

FIGURE 17: PROPAGANDA OF ANCIENT ROMAN WORLD

(SPQR - Senatus Populusque Romanus, meaning the Senate and Roman people)

FIGURE 18: ROMAN AQUILA

FIGURE 19: THE DOUBLE HEADED EAGLE IN ISLAMIC COIN POST SELJUK.
Nasir al-Din Mahmud, 1200 – 1222 AD.

FIGURE 20: VARIETY OF EAGLE INSIGNIAS FROM DIFFERENT EMPIRES

(sourced from Ancient Origin).

1. Double-headed Eagle from the Spanish Empire,
2. Double-headed Eagle from the Spanish Empire,
3. Double-headed Eagle from Holy Roman Empire,
4. Double-headed Eagle from Holy Roman Empire,
5. Double-headed Eagle from the Russian Empire.
6. Eagle of Saladin,
7. Eagle from the New Kingdom of Granada,
8. Eagle from the New Kingdom of Granada,
9. Eagle from the German Empire,
10. Eagle from Polish–Lithuanian Commonwealth

The symbols of the single or double-headed Eagle, with sometimes a lion resting on its chest, are also in use as borne by many nations' Coat of Arm/national emblems. The frequent use of Eagle in many national flags or Coat of Arms is also a sign of the colonial prowess of Great Britain

Chapter Ten

BEHOLD THE OLD, BUT NOW EARTH NEW MASTER

When the past is adequately reviewed, and the essential landmarks are well understood and accurately reestablished, it becomes easy to fully comprehend the symbols that hitherto stare humankind in the face without apparent meaning. In the American Great Seal - the obverse and reverse side clearly show the connection between the Eagle, on one side, and the pyramids of Egypt (many pyramids are also scattered across the globe), on the other side. The pyramid of Egypt is the home of the pharaohs who wore a serpent on their headgear as their distinct insignia. The "eye of providence" indicates that the high and mighty of this world is promoting a singular agenda – the close monitoring of everything and everyone, for the total control of the Earth. The primary struggle is mainly between the two brothers, that is, the **Eagle** versus **Serpent**.

From all the information gathered so far, the Eagle (with the double-headed Eagle) and the Serpent (with the Dragon) are two brothers of the same family that colonized the Earth a long time ago. The Eagle lineage has been in control for the past 2,000 years. Based on the precedents laid down in the past, the period from 1960 – 2000 was highly decisive as it denotes a possible change of baton between the two brothers; that is when the pendulum of world control would swing from the Eagle Clan back to the Serpent Clan. The big question is, was there anything that depicts a similitude of such a change in human history?

THE VATICAN SNAKEHEAD AUDITORIUM

The Paul VI Audience Hall is a building in Rome, named after Pope Paul the sixth who reigned from 1963 to 1978, with a seating capacity of 6,300. The building was designed by the Italian architect Pier Luigi Nervi who specialized in constructing large bunker-like structures. This particular building was a reinforced concrete completed in 1971, having been commissioned in 1963. The building capacity was, therefore, prepared to accommodate hundreds of '63' to commemorate the year in which the foundation was laid. This purpose-built edifice lies partially in Vatican City but mostly in Italy.

The aerial view of the roof shows a snake-like head with its mouth at one end and the two snake-slit-like-eyes on either side of the building. See figure 21 – 24 below. The stage also has two banisters that look like fangs, looking out to the audience with a long walkway path that looks like a giant snake tongue. A look from the front of the stage gives the impression that the Serpent has swallowed the audience. The Pope is seated in the very mouth of the serpent, in-between the two fangs and in front of the reptilian Jesus statue. When the pope addresses an audience, it gives the impression that he is speaking from the mouth of a giant serpent.

Pericle Fazzini created the massive bronze/copper-alloy reptilian Jesus sculpture named *La Resurrezione* (Italian for "The Resurrection"), claiming the idea depicts Christ "rising again from the explosion of this large olive grove, peaceful site of His last prayers. Christ rises from this crater torn open by a nuclear bomb, an atrocious explosion, a vortex of violence and energy." The hall lacks all symbols of Catholics, such as the crosses or the typical image of Jesus Christ. The Pope's Audience Hall depicts the feature of the Serpent rather than the God of the Bible. A valid question should rather be 'why was Jesus depicted as described above? Does it mean that the earth has been reserved for destruction with the use of the atomic bomb?

In the sculpture, the head of Jesus was turning into a serpent. The secret numerical symbol of the serpent, as derived from Genesis, is "33." Jesus Christ was also purported to have died at the age of "33." The eagle in the American Great Seal has 33 feathers on each wing to maintain stable flight; hence, 33 + 33 = **66**! Is it a coincidence that the statue of Jesus Christ in the Audience hall is **66 feet wide**? The Sphinx of Egypt is also **66 feet tall at the head!**

The observed synchronisms are clear messages and warnings to the Bible believers that the Age of Pisces, for which the story of Jesus Christ was designed, has come to the climax. A unified power has now been given to the old Sumerian and Egyptian warlord - Enki. The power of the Serpent, not of the misconstrued Satan or Lucifer, but the prince of Nibiru is here to rule again. Hence, the old warlord is back to power again to rule the earth. That is the story of the snakehead auditorium, as told by the masters at the Vatican. Only a fool will argue religious matters with the Vatican.

FIGURE 21: The Audience Hall aerial view when placed beside the serpent head showing the position of the eyes and the nostril (1).

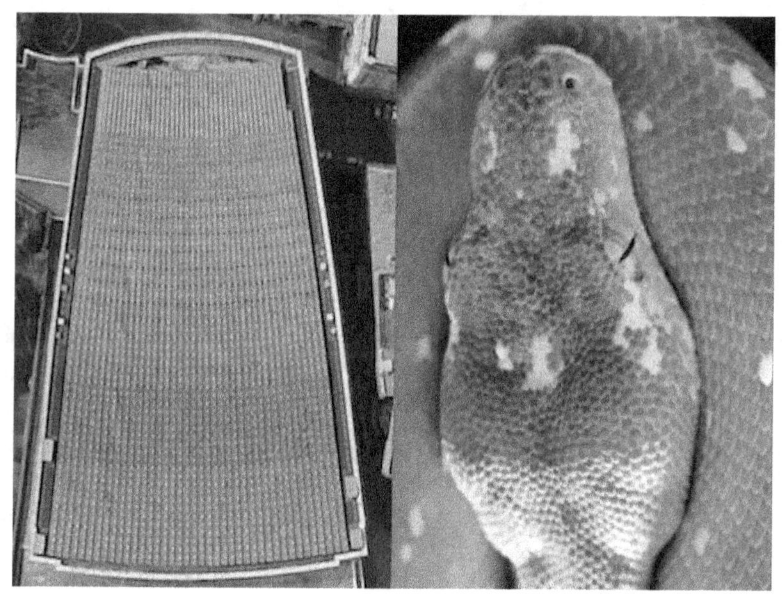

FIGURE 22: The Audience Hall aerial view when placed beside the serpent head showing the nostril and the eye (2).

FIGURE 23: The interior of the Audience Hall showing the eyes, the stage with the two fang-like banisters, and the tongue-like walkway.

FIGURE 24: The stage holding the massive 66 feet sculpture of Jesus Christ rising from a crater torn open by a nuclear bomb

Chapter Eleven

THE SECRET MESSAGE IN AMERICAN GREAT SEAL.[49]

FIGURE 25: THOMSON DRAWING IN 1782

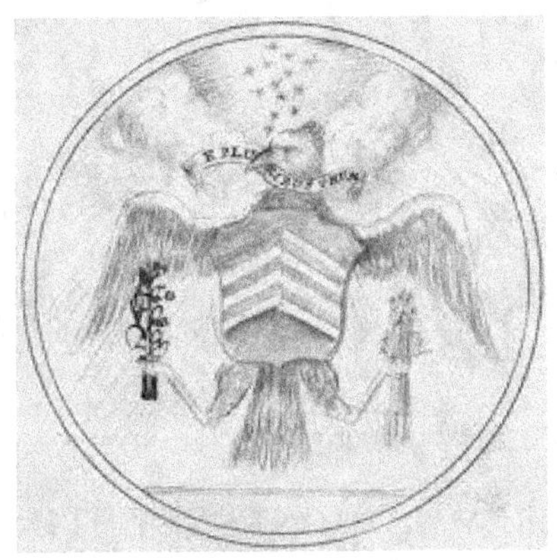

FIGURE 26: DRAWING MADE FROM LEWIS MOLD

---

[49] Images were sourced from Wikipedia

FIGURE 27: MASI TREATY-SEAL DIE OF 1825

FIGURE 28: A MARBLE SCULPTURE FROM ANCIENT ROMAN EMPIRE

The similarity between the last two pictures above is unmistaken. And to say that all the drawings were meant to mimic the marble sculpture would require little debate. The eagle and the scroll in the American Great Seal, in truth, depict the victory of the Eagle (clan) over the Serpent (clan) back in the days. The Masi treaty-seal die of 1825 perfectly replicates the marble, with a little adjustment. And the Thomson drawing of 1782 greatly influences what became the final impression of 1885 seen below.

FIGURE 29: UNITED STATE OF AMERICA SEAL (OBVERSE)

FIGURE 30: UNITED STATE OF AMERICA SEAL (REVERSE)

The American Great Seal of today evolved with different symbols incorporated at different times. In the latest design, which has remained almost unchanged since 1885, the Eagle was no longer gripping the scroll (serpent) by the neck but is gracefully carrying it in the middle. This would portray that the time of strife when the Eagle (family) first snatched the reign over the earth from the Serpent (family) was over. At the time of the drawings, the Eagle, as represented by British-America Empire, knew that it was just a matter of a few centuries before it relinquishes power back to his brother, the Serpent.

It is now clear that in riddles and symbols, those who knew the earth's real story speak, but only a few people understood. The "GOD" in whom the American founding fathers' trust is well presented in the Eagle and the Serpent (the scroll) of the seal – the emblem of the two Anunnaki brothers. The Eagle and obelisk are signs of ownership, and they boast of owing everything. With the use of the Mayan calendar, the decline of the UK-US Empire sets in as far back as December 21, 2012. It is expected that by 2300 CE, a New World Order should be fully operational. Here is the world mystery finally unveiled.

Chapter Twelve

THE FINAL THOUGHTS

I have put together my interpretation of the meaning of the Vatican snakehead auditorium. This edifice, simply put, is a modern-day physical attestation to the incredible story hitherto told about the ancient astronauts who, from heaven to earth, came and became the gods and goddesses unto humankind. The numerous ancient visitors of different species are the brain behind the long lost ancient civilisations. The many great monuments and ancient structures are the telltales left behind, which do not fit into the human evolution theory or creation story of Adam and Eve.

The construction of the serpent head auditorium marks the transmission of power from the lineage of Enlil (Eagle) back to Enki (Serpent). This is an ancient secret only known to those that mattered. In THEY LIED TO US, I called the human accomplices working hand in hand with the Anunnaki - the KEEPPer of secrets. Some of these human accomplices are believed to be Anunnaki hybrids. Hence, they are commonly referred to as people of the royal bloodline. These hybrids are said to be capable of shape-shifting. That is, at an instance, they can transform themselves from a human being into a reptilian. Some are said to shape-shift uncontrollably anytime they are angry or offended or under emotional stress. In order words, the Anunnaki are very much around us today, and they call the shots across the globe. They are said to regard the earth as their estate.

Many great philosophers, including Plato, knew these secrets, and he, in particular, subtly shared the truth in the allegory of the cave. Human beings live in a conditioned and controlled reality where religious induced miracles, innovations, technologies, etc. are masterminded, brought to earth, or created in secret temples, shrines, or laboratories. These 'innovations' are then adopted for human use and shared under a regulated system. The masses are not expected to know many things; hence, the government or/and the people in charge openly deny the truth while falsehood is promoted to the highest heaven using the different platforms created for such propaganda. The masses are only permitted to know what is approved to be revealed.

The Americans' motto is IN GOD WE TRUST. Hitherto, people are misled to imagine that the "GOD" herein referred to is either the Yahweh of the Jews, or Jesus Christ of the Christianity, or the Holy Trinity. Nothing can be farther from the truth than this illusion. The "GOD" that the founding fathers of the Americans refer to is clearly and cleverly encrypted in the symbols and numerology found on the Great seal.

The idea that God is ONE was fabricated to indoctrinate the masses and streamline human's whoring after the many deities of old. The problem is not just in the name or the holy land that craves pilgrimages — Jerusalem, Rome, Mecca, or the headquarters (campsites) of the various churches and religious bodies founded worldwide. The problem at hand is the separations of humans along the religious line and the ensuing disunity. Many take religious stories very literally, believing that every element concealed in it is accurate and that every written word was inspired. They seek for the best interpretations of the symbols and parables as contained therein. They plan and live their lives by the principles laid out for the believers, and nothing outside the holy book makes any meaning to them. To speak contrary to the content of the Scripture is considered anathema. To attempt to wake up humans from the state of ignorance and forgetfulness would be resisted.

Some are extremists, and it never crossed their minds that the religions they fastened their faith upon could ever have been forged or fabricated with the main character, such as Jesus Christ, never existed. If Jesus never lived, who lied to the prophet from Arabia. Many are unaware that beliefs were never designed or created to unite humankind but separate everyone into pockets of separatists who would take a portion of the supposedly holy book and attempt to create a global view from the contradictory statements therein.

Naturally, the dissociations and separations weaken true brotherhood as the emerging groups are likely to claim a position of superiority above the others. One person sees his or her 'God' and religion as greater or bigger than the others. When one has successfully amassed a sizeable wealth, he or she sees it as the benefits derived from the service he or she has rendered unto God – deservingly or undeservingly. Religions teach men that they are worthless without God and that they do not deserve to live or be in sustainable good health or success except for God's divine protection, guidance, and provision. Everyone merely complies with the norms than to become sub-creators that they were meant to be.

The profession of faith or oath-taking binds every member into a fraternity. Help is rendered *first* to the members of the 'household of faith.' Cohesion and loyalty are stronger among people of the same faith or denominations who often treat one another as members of occult groups. Therefore, there is no end at sight to human division and segregation. Humanity must come off the hook and begin to share a universal view, promoting global transformation wherein all things become ONE.

Just as many people will be reluctant to drop the fable of Adam and Eve in the Garden of Eden and that the Jews are a unique race favoured by God, so are many others who are unwilling to drop their faith or ethnic-based indoctrinations. Our minds have been transfused with the notion that we are wise while others are fools or that we know better than others. We fail to see greatness and potentials in others, which, when harnessed, can propel exponential growth. The earlier we all admit that we all grope in the dark of ignorance, pleasure, and self-centeredness, the better we attain awakening. The earlier we acknowledge that the distribution of knowledge and skills among humankind was hitherto skewed to favor some particular ethnic groups or races above the others, the better we realise the potential in all of us and the need to come together as one. The real test of human bravery lies in our ability to unlearn the many falsehoods so far fed into our minds, consciously and unconsciously.

Religion syncretism had been with humanity for as long as the human mind was sharpened to the high state of consciousness. The upgrade of the earliest forms of hominids to modern man made it possible for humankind to acquire higher intelligence. This, in return, made the infusion of the high-level soul into the intelligent minds possible – something the other primates do not possess. Thus, humans became a tertiary creator capable of probing and mimicking the work of the infinite creator. In the connecting chains are various levels of creators and sub-creator.

Modern researches have proven that the soul survives after death to confirm an age-long belief among the traditionalists. If this is so, one can as well conclude that the very part of humankind that lives on after death had consistently been 'alive' before birth. Hence, souls are immortal. If this is a fact and valid, then the resurrection theory peddled by religious propagandists is a fraud. Once an individual dies, he or she journeys 'home' to be given a warm welcome. The earth's mission is reviewed, and decisions are taken depending on the outcome of the careful assessment of the trip. If there is the need to make a return journey, this would be carried out as required. If there is the need to attend special classes before a return trip is embarked upon, the right decisions are made in the best interest of the parties involved. Some are promoted, some are demoted, and some remain on the same hierarchy. Findings show that reincarnation or metempsychosis (Greek) or transmig-ration or simply put "rebirth" is a natural soul experience.

As further expounded in THEY LIED TO US, the realm of the spirit is neither hell nor heaven; it is merely a HOME. Rebirth, therefore, is not a punishment but an opportunity to learn and relearn unique attributes and discharge tasks assigned to different individuals. It is essential to mention that the author's findings do not support the notion or belief that the soul of human reincarnates as a tree or stone or other animals. The line of separation between man and other physical entities cannot be crossed. Some human minds are a total reprobate, but the few cannot be taken to represent a whole. Hence, humanity cannot be said to be irredeemably wicked. Humans are of either good or bad characters and subject to external influences.

Further works also show that the presence of other contemporary beings or superior races in the universe should not continually be mistaken that they are gods and goddesses or demigods or demons and angels. Humankind must carefully study the characters and natures of various beings on the earth, in the near-earth space, and in the universe as a whole, to devise how we can co-exist with mutual respect and possibly make dealings for the betterment of the human race.

The divide and rule scheme hitherto in place to scuttle unity among human races should be rendered ineffective. We must preserve the integrity of the earth, and there must be a truce and agreement by whatever means among human races. In religion, the truth is that there was never any person born of a virgin and called Jesus Christ in the first century. No saviour came and died for the sins of the world. This was an ideology borrowed from Egypt and

Africa, where human minds were probably at the highest level of consciousness a long time before the Age of Pisces. Behind the religious activities are real unseen players, cheering, yelling, or groaning.

The messianic idea was only rebranded by the Romans to create a new religion to rule the New Age. The use of the term anti-Christ to describe anyone who stands against the supposition that there was ever a historical Jesus the Christ in the first century is, to say the least, very treacherous. How can anyone be against something that never existed? The concept of a 'Christ' or 'the anointed one' who would help the masses to cope with the challenges of life is age-long and mostly suitable for the feebleminded, but it remains what it is – a myth. A close friend recently agrees that religion was created to control human excesses; to create a morally stable society. I agree with this *in toto*. It amounts to asking for too much when people began to promote that religion brings salvation. Salvation from what, from an imaginary Adam and Eve's sins? This is very ridiculous.

The individual and collective states of consciousness go a long way to determine what every individual and society would have the capacity to accept, ingest, and practice. The Bible and Qur'an erred that God created Adam and Eve in a garden somewhere in Mesopotamia around 3,760 BCE. The Qur'an, in particular, is vague since there are no sufficient data or information to confirm or deny various claims and probably put a date on when certain events happened. This was intentionally put in place to save it from the likes of attacks persistently made against the Bible. Since the Garden of Eden is a myth, so is the story of a supposed saviour who came to "save that which was (supposedly) lost"[50] in that fabulous Garden.
The ancient text mentions that there was a Deluge on earth circa 13,000 years ago, after which King Anu of

---

[50] Matthew 18:11, Luke 19:10

Nibiru divided the earth among his two sons. The ancient Egyptians called themselves 'people of Anu,' and it is reported that even in the Far East, some tribes call themselves people of "Ainu." Enki, with possible human assistants, is said to have a great specialty in building massive ships to travel, explore and map out the globe. Hence, the evidence of the human presence in very remote places of the earth dated to ancient times and long before the voyage of Columbus is a possibility. From available facts, the Anunnaki gave civilisation to humankind with the appointment of human kings only from the beginning of the Sumerian and Egyptian (human) civilisations or the first dynasty. Before that period, the Anunnaki and possibly the remnants of a long lost ancient civilisation were the deities, the rulers, the Kings and Queens over the earth.

There was a change in the leadership of Nibiru in the 14th century,[51] and Nanna, the moon-god of old, replaced Anu as the King. The new leadership reviewed the case of the Jews and reinstated them into the mainstream of human history. Since then, the Jews had been under the protective arms of the British-America Empire. How did the change in leadership affect the coloured races and, most significantly, the black race? The book THEY LIED TO US says it all.

The declaration made by the construction of the snakehead auditorium at the Vatican implies that the Papal seat takes order from a higher power – the Anunnaki. Ordinarily, the white supremacists would never want the coloured races to have a clue that the pendulum is swinging to their favour. The Age of Aquarius [2300 – 4460 CE] is a promising era where the water of knowledge will generously be poured forth. It is good news for the black and other coloured races. Just as the Jews were once brutalised and persecuted before the global reconciliation,

---

[51] See chapter sixteen of THEY LIED TO US.

the moment for the full reconciliation of the black race is here. The white race was favoured by a fraction of the Anunnaki, who had a say in how the Piscean age should be governed. In their wisdom, they chose to promote the white race above the others. The white race was, *ab initio*, never stronger or better than the black race or the other races. No, not all; it was The Power That Be that decided to trade places with the black race in the Age of Pisces for the white race. It was a criminal decision, very offensive and demoralising, considering the psychological effects on the races that were dehumanised. However, nothing better should be expected of the reptilian masters that are naturally cold-blooded and lack empathy; they see and use human beings as pawns. They work behind the scene as the "Hidden Hand" or "Deep State."

From what I have put together about the true origin of the human soul in my other book, THEY LIED TO US, everything in existence at the soul level is ONE. The Anunnaki never created the soul (spirit and mind); this came from the Infinite Creator, whose origin and personality remains a mystery. The souls that exist at a much higher plane could reveal what GOD or the highest authorities in the spirit realms are, but alas, such privileged information may not be known because such souls no longer reincarnate to earth.

The Infinite Creator was never Yahweh, nor Jesus Christ or part of any Trinity or Allah of the Qur'an or the Hindu or traditional deities; the Infinite Creator is far and above each and all the religions. Taking a cue from the six blind men who visit the elephant, no single religion can represent GOD. GOD became everything - the living and non-living things. We are all infinitesimal fractions of GOD, yet GOD remains unchanged. Only those who are truly awakened to truth can tap into and utilize many of the mysteries of the universe. As said earlier, Jesus is not coming back the second time because he was never here the first time.

The danger facing humanity, under the current condition and situation, is that almost everyone will continue to clutch unto one end of the religious stick. Almost everyone would believe his religion is right and rewarding, but others are in the dark and satanic. Almost everyone would believe in at least one holy book, unquestionably. And many others are perplexed at the contradictory religious beliefs and presentations, and they would choose not to be bothered, believing in nothing. I hope that my books would provide sufficient ground for easy review of human history and various religious practices.

If my work is true that some smart guys, either human or extraterrestrial, or a hybrid started the movement to change human belief form polytheism and pantheism to monotheism some 2500 years ago, then the human mind has been successfully tamed. We have no God to harm if we intelligently reconsider our religious stands; we most probably only have our ego to bruise. As long as people are being killed for presumed religious blasphemy, the human mind is still veiled. As long as some superpower nations would wreck the global economy and ruin the lives of millions of people, then we need to identify the driving force. Humanity must come together to share knowledge and collectively protect the earth. As long as humans incarnate and reincarnate on this planet, society owes it as a duty to make the earth an Eden, a Park of Pleasure. God will never do this; only humans can come together to get the job done.

Science will continue to explore and report their findings to expand our knowledge about how the universe work. No one needs to go to Jerusalem, Rome, or Mecca in search of GOD. GOD is here, and everywhere is 'here.' We are in the universe, and the universe is in us. When we love one another unconditionally, we become one with God, and God's divine plan is revealed in everything seen and unseen. The primary assignment of every human is not to search for and worship God but to know oneself and the purpose of his existence.

When we are told to hate or kill others, what we were never told was that when we act wickedly, we stain our Karma and retard our soul journey. When we commit crimes, we are forced into an alliance with hostile spiritual powers. Such partnerships bind us to the earth realm as slaves. We must strive to become genuinely awakened and make decisions that will help us evolve above prejudice, superstitions, evil, humanmade religions, ethnicity, racial biases, etc. Each man bears and repays the injury he causes — whatever we sow, we reap. The so-called confession of sin and automatic forgiveness is a blatant lie. Such do not earn salvation though it may help to deal with heavy guilt for the past wrongdoings. Every soul must learn to let the good deeds overwhelmingly overshadow all evil. As much as we can, we must push evil out of human existence. It is possible to create heaven on earth. Though GOD never wrote a book but selected ancient wisdom is preserved in some 'holy books.' We can choose to adopt the good things in the books and reject everything anti-human to encourage the divide and rule scheme. Many teachings in the holy books predispose humans to abuse, suppression, and lack of initiatives. Violence and wars have become the trademarks of religious intolerance. Let humanity come together and reason together to become wise, eliminating evil. Let us all live in true, unconditional LOVE.

INDEX

www.ingramcontent.com/pod-product-compliance
Lightning Source LLC
Chambersburg PA
CBHW070534160726

48003CB00004B/1783